HOW TO COOK LIKE
A JEWISH MOTHER

HOW TO COOK LIKE
A JEWISH MOTHER

by June Roth

illustrated by Rob Cobuzio

CASTLE BOOKS

In memory of Isaac Spiewak,
and to the family who proudly bear his name.
May his wisdom be perpetuated.

CONTENTS

"She looketh well to the ways of her household,
And eateth not the bread of idleness."

BOOK OF PROVERBS

How To Tell a
Jewish Mother

Scratch a Jewish mother and you will find a tiger underneath! She is fiercely protective of her family and their welfare. She forages the best food for them, and prepares it with traditional skills. She maketh them to dine well at her table. She provideth loving food for their bodies and books of culture for their minds. She proddeth her children through schools, while binding them to their heritage with hoops of homemade noodles. She careth for their ills with pots of rich chicken soup, and chaseth away their troubles with strudel and blintzes. Surely goodness and mercy shall follow her family all the days of her life, as she strives to bring forth sustenance from her bountiful table.

A Jewish mother zealously guards her recipes. Indeed, she rarely writes them down. She cooks with a handful of this and a handful of that, and somehow she has been blessed with just the right-sized hands.

In Yiddish, she is called a *balabusta*, which means a woman who runs an efficient household. She learned the art of homemaking from her mother, and she will teach it to her daughter.

She is a survivor. She represents over five thousand years of heritage and laws of a people who endured slavery and wandered the world over, until at last they reached their Promised Land. Her repertoire of Jewish menus reflects the history and geographical movements of her people.

From Hungary comes the goulash and the strudel; from Germany the kugels; from Russia the cabbage and beet soups; from Poland the *farfel* and kasha dishes; from Austria the tortes; from Holland the butter cakes; from France the addition of wines to cooking; from England the love of fish; from Spain the olives and cooking oils; from the Middle East the ginger and cinnamon in meat dishes; and from America the abundance and variety of poultry, meats, and vegetables. Put them all together and you have an unusual collection of gourmet dishes which have been adapted to kosher rules and passed down from generation to generation.

Kosher rules are the Jewish dietary laws which involve restrictions laid down in the Old Testament. Simply stated, they set these limitations:

Do not mix milk or milk products with meat or meat products in the same dish or at the same meal.

Only the forequarters of animals that have cloven hooves and chew the cud may be used for food after the humane supervision of their slaughter.

Fish must have fins and scales; all others may not be eaten.

Poultry must be slaughtered according to humane and ritual laws.

Birds of prey, birds that are shot, and birds that have died of natural causes may not be used.

Food is divided into two categories, *milchig* (dairy) and *fleishig* (meat), which must not be served together at the same meal. Neutral foods, called *pareve*, consisting of vegetables, fruits, fish, cereal, or eggs, may be served with either a *milchig* or *fleishig* meal.

Religious Jewish people have two sets of dishes and utensils, keeping one set for *milchig* foods and the other for *fleishig* foods. These utensils are washed separately, with a soap free of animal fats, and dried with separate towels. A kosher kitchen may have one dishwasher with two sets of racks, one electric mixer with two sets of beaters and bowls, and one electric blender with two sets of attachments and jars.

A traditional Jewish mother observes all of these rules, a modern Jewish mother may or may not and yet she maintains her home in other customary styles. Her career is her family and she devotes herself to creating a warm, happy family life. She is both proud and generous, and uses her homemaking skills to promote the well-being of her husband and children. Her dining table is the magnetic field that draws all the members of her family together, no matter their ages. Despite the advice of psychiatrists who prevail on all mothers to learn to let go of their children, a Jewish mother never lets go. True, if she is wise, she slackens the rein with one hand, while with the other, she stirs the traditional meals that bring her children and her children's children home to the comfort of her table and to the good food that "only Mama knows how to make."

· 2 ·

"Every wise woman buildeth her house;
But the foolish plucketh it down with her own hands."

BOOK OF PROVERBS

You've Got To Have *Tam*

One simple factor distinguishes the *balabusta* from the aspiring Jewish cook. It is called *tam*. *Tam* literally means good taste, but with reference to Jewish cooking, it means the right taste.

Since Jewish cooking is affected by geographical heredity, there are many disagreements on what constitutes the right taste. For example, cooks of Russian origin prefer their fish to be peppery, while those of Polish background prefer their fish to be sweet. Some *balabustas* say that matzo balls should be light and fluffy; others insist that they be hard. Every major recipe will be challenged by someone who has a different (and better) way to make it. Right or wrong by geographical standards, the recipes in this book have been selected for their authenticity and for their *tam*.

You will notice that many recipes have long lists of ingredients and some involved procedures. There are few shortcuts to achieving *tam*, yet where they are available, they have, of course, been included. However, if you want to cook like a Jewish mother, you have to be prepared to add the special ingredients that give a dish its own special *tam*. Remember, too, that rich tastes require rich ingredients, so do not tamper with the amounts of eggs and butter in the recipes and expect to get the same results.

Getting authentic recipes involves quite a bit of persuasion. After that it usually takes a good deal of sleuthing to find the "kicker" ingredient that has been left out. Since these recipes are rarely written down by real *balabustas*, but are handed down from memory, there are times when they forget to tell you the single ingredient that will make a truly great dish instead of a good imitation. So be sure to add the bits of dill, the sugar, and the ginger, even when they seem to appear in strange places. It is likely that you are adding the "kicker" that gives the dish its *tam*.

It is interesting to trace the lists of ingredients back to the geographical origin of each recipe, and to note that certain combinations were due to the availability of products in a given area. You will also find the same ingredients used over and over again in slightly different ways—perhaps with one change in seasoning or a different method of cooking. The hearty peasant dishes reveal great ingenuity. Having to use the same ingredients might have made for monotonous fare, but the imagination of the cook saved the day and she created new and delicious taste experiences.

There are few bland dishes in Jewish cooking, although you will find many with tender, subtle flavors. The use of savory vegetables, onions, garlic, and fruit lends distinct piquancy to traditional meals. Frequently delightful taste sensations are achieved by combining hot and cold in the same plate, such as the hot potato in the bowl of cold borscht, or the cold sour cream with the hot potato *latkes*.

As a side line, the Jewish cook practices a little medicine too. A tablespoonful of zesty horseradish will clear your sinuses in a hurry, and a heavy hand with garlic will guarantee a burning fire in your chest for hours. She cures all ills with chicken soup and a glass of tea. Whether it is the soup or the tender care that works the wonders, we can only guess, but chicken soup promoted speedy recoveries long before penicillin came along.

Open the kitchen cupboard of a Jewish cook and you will discover a variety of spices and herbs from all over the world. Ginger, cinnamon, nutmeg, bay leaf, dill, and parsley are her favorites in addition to the staples: salt, pepper, and paprika. You will also find potato flour, matzo meal, and peanut oil, ingredients common to many Jewish dishes. *Schmaltz* (chicken fat), with its distinctive flavor and thin consistency, is the taste factor in many recipes. It is rendered with onions from the fat of the fowl used for chicken soup, and it is usually stored in a tightly covered jar in the refrigerator.

Cabbages, onions, beets, and potatoes are the staple vegetables because they were generally plentiful in central Europe where millions of Jewish people were settled for several centuries. Russian, Polish, and Hungarian dishes in particular call for these vegetables.

Along with butter, eggs, and milk, *smetana* (sour cream) is used liberally. It appears in fish dishes, on dairy offerings, and many times in coffee cakes and other rich doughs. Sour cream is traditionally offered with borscht, blintzes, *latkes, verenikes,* and salad bowls, which consist mainly of cucumbers, radishes, and tomatoes. It is the crowning touch on fresh berries and a must for topping a bowl of cottage cheese.

Nuts and dried fruits, *lekvar* (prune filling), poppy seeds, honey, and brown sugar are other ingredients which play a prominent role in Jewish cuisine.

All these items contribute to the *tam* that makes a Jewish mother's cooking remembered with mouth-watering nostalgia. They will start you on your way to mastering the art of Jewish cookery.

· 3 ·

Every Little Dish
Has a Reason All Its Own

The Sabbath and the principal Jewish holidays have distinctive menus which are repeated all around the world in tradition-observing Jewish homes. The family perpetuates its religious heritage not only by ritual prayers but also by dining in a customary way.

The Sabbath, a weekly observance, begins at sundown on

Friday and ends at sundown on Saturday. On Friday evening the Jewish mother sets her table with a clean white cloth, her finest china and silver. She blesses the two white candles and places two loaves of challah (egg bread) before her family. The two loaves are symbolic of the double serving of manna which fell from heaven the day before the Sabbath during the Exodus from Egypt. The classic Friday night dinner includes chicken soup and boiled or roasted chicken. Frequently guests are invited to share the festive dinner, whose menu might be:

Gefilte Fish with Beet Horseradish
Chicken Soup with Noodles
Roast Chicken
Potato *Tzimmes*
Carrots and Peas
Challah
Wine
Apple Strudel
Tea

Following the rules for no work or cooking on the Sabbath, the menu for the noonday Saturday meal includes a *cholent* which has been cooking and perfuming the air with its savory aroma since the afternoon before. *Cholent* is a favorite Sabbath dish because its flavor is not impaired by long, slow cooking.

Gefilte Fish with Beet Horseradish
or Chopped Herring
Cholent
Fruit Compote
Sliced Sponge Cake
Tea

Rosh Hashanah, the start of the Jewish New Year, occurs in late September or in early October. It marks the beginning of a ten-day period of spiritual self-analysis, penitence, and prayer. It is also a time to serve sweet dishes, such as honey and apple slices, symbolizing man's hope for a "sweet" year of happiness and fulfillment. A typical Rosh Hashanah dinner might include:

Sliced Apples dipped in Honey
Gefilte Fish with Beet Horseradish
Chicken Soup with *Mandlen*
Roast Duck or Chicken, with *Farfel* Stuffing
Yam *Tzimmes*
Green Beans
Honey Cake
Tea

Yom Kippur, the Day of Atonement, is a day of fasting from sundown the night before to sunset. On Yom Kippur the Jew repents for his sins, seeking a reconciliation with the Almighty and petitioning for a year of health, happiness, and peace. Yom Kippur culminates the ten holy days starting with Rosh Hashanah. During this entire period sweet dishes, especially those made with honey and fruit, are traditionally served. The dinner to break the fast at sunset is likely to include:

Chopped Herring
Chicken Soup with *Kreplach*
Roast Beef or Chicken
Stuffed Derma
Glazed Carrots
Apple-Matzo Crumb Cake or *Teiglach*
Tea

Sukkoth, a holiday similar to Thanksgiving, is celebrated by a seven-day period of feasting to give thanks for the good harvest. It occurs directly after Yom Kippur. An air of festiveness marks this holiday and bountiful meals which emphasize the products of the fall season are served:

Stuffed Cabbage
Mushroom Barley Soup
Roast Chicken or Duck
Apple-Noodle Pudding
Green Beans
Strudel or Fruit Compote
Tea

Chanukah, which is also known as the Festival of Lights, takes place in late November or in early December and lasts for eight days. It commemorates the second-century struggle of the Jewish people against the oppression of the King of Syria. Led by Judas Maccabeus and his brothers, the Jews were victorious in regaining the right to worship in their Temple in Jerusalem. One day's supply of oil miraculously burned for eight days. In Jewish homes today, Chanukah candles are lit each day in remembrance of the religious freedom gained so long ago. One of the most joyous holidays, Chanukah is celebrated by giving gifts to children, playing games, singing, and enjoying the warmth of family life. Following the instructions for the holiday it is also a time to "eat and be merry." Here is a typical menu for the family gathering:

Chopped Liver

Chicken Soup with *Kreplach*

Roast Duckling with Orange-Prune Stuffing

Potato *Latkes*

Applesauce

Green Peas

Sponge Cake

Tea

Purim, a one-day festive holiday, usually occurs in March. It commemorates the defeat of Haman's efforts to destroy the Jews in Persia. The Purim table is customarily laden with many good things. The specialty is the dessert, a stuffed three-cornered cookie called *hamantaschen*. At a Purim dinner the following dishes might be served:

Chopped Herring

Cabbage Soup

Stuffed Breast of Veal

Pineapple *Kugel*

Green Beans

Hamantaschen

Tea

Pesach, or Passover, commemorates the Exodus of the Jews from their slavery in Egypt. Family and friends gather around the table for a symbolic dinner, a Seder, to recall the history of their people's escape to freedom. Only unleavened products may be used during this eight-day holiday. Matzo is used instead of bread, matzo meal and potato flour are substituted for regular flour, and only eggs are used for leavening. The Seder dinner is served after the family has read the Haggadah, the narrative of the Exodus which contains the Seder ritual, and informed the children present of the history of the holiday. The table is laid beautifully, and according to custom there is a large Passover plate which contains:

A roasted lamb bone, in the upper right-hand corner, which represents the Paschal lamb.

A roasted egg, in the upper left-hand corner, which represents an ancient offering.

Moror, usually symbolized by horseradish, a bitter herb, placed in the center of the plate, signifying the bitterness of slavery.

Charoseth, a paste of diced apples, nuts, and wine, in the lower right-hand corner, symbolizing the clay and bricks used by the slaves to build cities for the Pharaoh.

Parsley or watercress, the sweet herbs, placed in the lower left-hand corner of the plate, which represent spring and the future.

Salt water in bowls around the table, for the tears shed by the enslaved people.

A wine glass at each place setting is filled four times during the reading of the Haggadah.

Three whole pieces of matzo are wrapped in separate cloth napkins and arranged one atop the other on a plate before the leader of the Seder. The center matzo will be hidden before the meal is finished, and the lucky child who finds it will be paid a ransom for his good fortune.

The traditional dinner is served this way:

Hard-Cooked Egg with Salt Water
Gefilte Fish with Beet Horseradish
Chicken Soup with *Knaidlach*

Roast Chicken with Matzo Stuffing
Carrot Fruit *Tzimmes*
Asparagus
Passover Sponge Cake
Tea

For the second night of Seder, the menu might be:

Chopped Liver
Hot Beef Borscht
Brisket Pot Roast
Plain *Tzimmes*
Spinach
Matzo Honey Cake
Tea

Shavuoth, a two-day holiday in late May or early June, honors the Torah, the basic law of the Jews. It commemorates the time when Moses received the Ten Commandments on Mount Sinai. Emphasis is customarily placed upon dairy foods. Here is a typical Shavuoth menu:

Potato Soup
Sweet and Sour Fish
Milchig Stuffed Cabbage
Green Beans
Blintzes with Sour Cream
Cream Cheese *Rugelach*
Tea or Coffee

It becomes apparent that food is an integral part of the home observance of Jewish holidays, with special dishes that are the same today as they have been for countless generations. A mother who learns to prepare these menus participates in the time-honored traditions of her people, and binds her family together around the warmth and goodness of the dining table.

· 4 ·

"A virtuous woman is a crown to her husband;
But she that doeth shamefully is as rottenness in his bones."

BOOK OF PROVERBS

A Little Something To Start

A *forshpeis* or appetizer is served in very small portions since it
is designed to whet the appetite, not satisfy it. Although usually
considered the first dinner course, appetizers are also served with
cocktails before dinner. Today, many favorites such as herring
in sour cream sauce, herring in wine sauce, pickled salmon,
chopped liver, and chopped eggplant are available in Jewish deli-

catessens or in jars at your local supermarket. This chapter has recipes for homemade delicacies, and others, listed as main courses in succeeding chapters, can be served in smaller portions as a *forshpeis*, too.

Not included here are the grapefruit halves, melon wedges, and other fruit appetizers which start a meal equally well. Many Jewish mothers do, in fact, begin important meals with a serving of fresh fruit before the special *forshpeis*. These meals, however, are intended to last for several hours and to be enjoyed leisurely.

Whatever the occasion, appetizers will stimulate your taste buds and sharpen your appetite for the good things that follow.

RED CAVIAR DIP

1 *pint sour cream*
1 *3-ounce package chive cream cheese*

1 *small jar red caviar*

Mash chive cream cheese into sour cream. Add red caviar and blend carefully, trying not to mash the roe. Serve as a dip with crackers.
Makes about 2½ cups.

LOX DIP

1 *cup sour cream*
1 *3-ounce package cream cheese*

⅛ *pound lox*

Place sour cream, mashed cream cheese, and lox in a blender and blend at low speed until the mixture is combined. Add chopped chives or grated onion if desired. Serve as a cracker dip.
Makes about 1½ cups.

SARDINE PUFFS

2 *egg whites, stiffly beaten*
1 *cup mayonnaise*
1 *cup mashed boneless*
  sardines

¼ *teaspoon salt*
⅛ *teaspoon pepper*
Melba rounds
Paprika

Blend mayonnaise into stiffly beaten egg whites. Add mashed sardines. Season with salt and pepper. Pile mixture on melba rounds; sprinkle tops with paprika. Broil for 3 minutes, or until puffed up and lightly browned. Serve hot with cold drinks. *Makes about 3 dozen.*

KNISHELACH

1 *large onion, diced*
3 *tablespoons chicken fat or*
  pareve margarine
½ *pound liver, broiled and*
  ground
3 *cups cooked mashed*
  potatoes
2 *eggs, slightly beaten*

2 *tablespoons chicken fat or*
  pareve margarine
1 *teaspoon salt*
⅛ *teaspoon pepper*
6 *tablespoons matzo meal*
1 *egg yolk, beaten with*
  1 *tablespoon water*

Sauté onion in the 3 tablespoons fat. Combine with ground liver and season with salt and pepper to taste.

Combine mashed potatoes with eggs, 2 tablespoons fat, salt, pepper, and matzo meal. Form into walnut-sized balls. Make a depression in the center of each and fill with liver mixture. Brush with diluted egg yolk. Place on a well-greased baking sheet and bake in a hot oven (400 degrees) for 20 minutes, or until well browned. *Makes about 3½ dozen.*

POTATO PUFFS

¼ *ounce dry yeast*
1 *tablespoon lukewarm water*
1¾ *cups flour, sifted*
¼ *pound butter*
½ *teaspoon salt*

1½ *teaspoons sugar*
1 *egg, separated*
1 *tablespoon vinegar*
½ *cup evaporated milk*
2 *cups mashed potatoes*

Stir yeast into water and set aside. Combine flour, butter, salt, and sugar into a crumbly mixture. Add egg yolk, vinegar, and evaporated milk to the yeast mixture. Combine mixtures into a dough, forming a large ball. Place dough in a greased bowl, cover with a clean cloth, and let rise for one hour, or refrigerate for at least eight hours.

Cut dough in quarters. Roll each section ¼ inch thick into a 3-inch-by-10-inch rectangle. Spread ½ cup of mashed potatoes down the center of each rectangle, the long way. Fold each side over the center and pinch the ends closed. Place the four long filled rolls on a greased cookie sheet. Brush tops with egg white. Bake at 350 degrees for 20 minutes, or until lightly browned. Cut in 1-inch slices.
Makes 4 dozen.

POTATO-CHEESE VERENIKES

Homemade Noodle Dough (see page 35):
1 *cup farmer cheese*
½ *cup mashed potatoes*
1 *onion, sautéed*

½ *teaspoon salt*
¼ *teaspoon pepper*
Melted butter

Make noodle dough as described on page 35. Roll out and cut into 4-inch rounds. To make the filling: Combine the mashed farmer cheese with the mashed potatoes and add the onion, salt, and pepper. Fill centers of the 4-inch noodle rounds, pinch the edges tightly closed, forming half-rounds. Drop the *verenikes*

into rapidly boiling salted water. When they rise to the top they are done. Scoop them out with a slotted spoon, drain briefly, and place in a buttered baking dish. Brush with melted butter and bake for 15 minutes in a 350-degree oven. Serve immediately with sour cream.
Makes 2 dozen.

FRIED CHICKEN BITS

2 *whole breasts of chicken*　　1 *cup chicken fat*
1 *egg*　　2 *tablespoons white horse-*
2 *tablespoons water*　　　*radish*
1 *cup fine bread crumbs*　　½ *cup orange marmalade*

Bone breasts of chicken and cut into 2-inch squares. Beat egg and add water. Dip chicken pieces, one at a time, into the egg, then into the bread crumbs. Heat chicken fat in a large skillet. Fry chicken bits in the hot fat until chicken is browned on all sides. Drain on paper toweling to remove excess fat. Combine horseradish and marmalade into a sauce. Place sauce in a dish in the center of a platter and surround with fried chicken bits.
Makes 2 dozen.

CHOPPED EGGPLANT

1 *whole eggplant*　　　½ *teaspoon salt*
1 *onion, sliced*　　　⅛ *teaspoon pepper*
1 *green pepper, cut up*　　1 *tablespoon lemon juice*
1 *tablespoon oil*

Bake whole eggplant in a 350-degree oven until skin is soft and wrinkled. Remove from oven and cut skin away. Chop in large chopping bowl. Add onion and green pepper and chop all very

fine. Add oil, salt, pepper, and lemon juice. Serve cold on lettuce as an appetizer, or serve with crackers as a spread.
Makes about 2 cups.

CHOPPED HERRING

1 *herring, preferably fresh or*   1 *apple, peeled and cored*
  matjes   2 *tablespoons vinegar*
2 *hard-cooked eggs*   ¼ *teaspoon pepper*
1 *onion, cut up*   1 *teaspoon sugar*

Soak the herring overnight; remove skin and bones, and clean. Chop herring, eggs, onion, and apple very fine. Add vinegar, pepper, and sugar. Garnish with black olives. Serve as first course or as a spread for crackers.
Makes about 2 cups.

CHOPPED LIVER*

1 *large onion, sliced*   2 *tablespoons chicken fat*
Chicken fat or oil   ½ *teaspoon salt*
1 *pound chicken livers*   ¼ *teaspoon pepper*
2 *hard-cooked eggs*

Sauté sliced onion in some chicken fat or oil over low heat until just golden. Add chicken livers and sauté 5 minutes on each side. Remove from skillet, place in a large chopping bowl, and add peeled hard-cooked eggs. Chop fine. Add 2 tablespoons chicken fat, salt, and pepper. Pile into a greased two-cup, shaped mold and refrigerate until serving time. Unmold, and serve surrounded with crackers for spreading, or serve scoops of chopped liver on lettuce as an appetizer course.
Makes about 2 cups.

* Kosher cooks must score and broil the liver before sautéing. Liver does not have to be salted and rinsed before cooking, but it must be quickly seared by broiling.

MOCK CHOPPED LIVER

2 cups cooked string beans, fresh or canned
2 hard-cooked eggs
1 onion, sliced
1 tablespoon chicken fat
½ teaspoon salt
¼ teaspoon pepper

Drain string beans and place in chopping bowl. Add peeled hard-cooked eggs. Sauté onion in chicken fat until golden; add to the chopping bowl. Chop all very fine. Season with salt and pepper. Add additional chicken fat if necessary to hold the mixture together. Spread on crackers.
Makes about 2½ cups.

GEFILTE FISH DIP

1 pint jar gefilte fish, drained
3 tablespoons gefilte fish juice
8 ounces cream cheese
1 teaspoon lemon juice
½ teaspoon salt
⅛ teaspoon pepper
2 teaspoons white horseradish

Mash gefilte fish. Blend together with fish juice. Mash cream cheese into the fish mixture. Add lemon juice, salt, pepper, and white horseradish. Chill in refrigerator about 1 hour. Place in a bowl in the center of a large tray, surrounded by matzo crackers.
Makes 3 cups.

HOME-TOUCH TINY FISH BALLS

1 1-pound jar miniature gefilte fish balls
½ cup matzo meal
1 cup peanut oil

Heat peanut oil in a skillet until hot but not smoking. Drain fish balls and roll in matzo meal. Place carefully in heated fat and fry until golden brown. Serve hot on toothpicks with Horseradish Dip.

Horseradish Dip:

¼ cup mayonnaise   ¼ cup red horseradish

Combine mayonnaise and horseradish. Serve with the Tiny Fish Balls.
Makes about 2 dozen.

CHERRY DUMPLINGS

1 8-ounce package farmer cheese
1 egg
½ teaspoon salt
1 tablespoon butter

2 large seeded rolls, soaked in milk
Flour
1 1-pound can sweet cherries, drained and pitted

Mash farmer cheese; add egg and salt. Add softened butter. Squeeze or press milk from rolls. Add to cheese mixture and blend into smooth dough, adding only as much flour as needed to make a soft but not sticky dough. Roll out ¼ inch thick, cut in squares, put a cherry in the center of each square, and gather ends together around the cherry, sealing them together on top. Boil in salted water for 5 minutes. Remove with a slotted spoon and serve hot with a dip of browned butter, sugar, and cinnamon.
Makes about 2 dozen.

POTATO DUMPLINGS WITH MARMALADE

4 or 5 large potatoes, peeled
  and grated
2 cups flour
½ teaspoon salt
3 egg yolks

Marmalade
½ cup hot butter
2 tablespoons poppy seeds
1 tablespoon sugar

Combine grated potatoes, flour, and salt. Add beaten egg yolks. Roll out ¼ inch thick, and cut into 2-inch-by-2-inch squares. Fill centers with marmalade, using 1 teaspoon per dumpling; pull all edges together at the top and pinch firmly to seal. Boil for 15 minutes in rapidly boiling water. Remove with a slotted spoon. Combine the hot melted butter with poppy seeds and sugar, and pour over hot potato dumplings.

Makes about 2½ dozen.

"She openeth her mouth with wisdom;
And the law of kindness is on her tongue."
BOOK OF PROVERBS

Jewish Penicillin
and Other Magic Brews

Believe it or not, Jewish mothers do make other soups besides their famous chicken soup. Soup is prepared in either *milchig* or *fleishig* style, depending on the type of meal for which it is intended. The *milchig* soups, which have milk and butter as their base, are usually a fish or vegetable concoction. They never contain beef or chicken. The *fleishig* soups have beef or beef bones as their base and many are hearty enough to be complete meals in themselves. Sometimes a *fleishig* soup is served first and then the soup meat, accompanied by a horseradish sauce, follows as the main dish.

The recipes in this chapter are designed to make good, stick-to-the-ribs soups. They will make a large pot of soup which will last for two days, so as to make the whole project worthwhile. Beet and cabbage soups especially seem to taste better the second day as their flavors "marry" each other with time.

BORSCHT

2 *bunches beets, scraped and sliced*	1 *teaspoon salt*
	3 *tablespoons sugar*
1 *onion, peeled and sliced*	*Juice of 2 lemons*
2 *quarts water*	½ *pint sour cream*

Put beets and sliced onion in a large saucepan. Add water, salt, sugar, and lemon juice. Bring to boil, then simmer until beets are tender. Put beets and onion through a sieve or a food mill and then return them to the soup. Chill. Serve with dollops of sour cream.
Serves 8.

Variations

1. Serve with freshly boiled hot potato.
2. Serve with peeled diced cucumber.
3. Serve with sliced hard-cooked egg.
4. To 1 quart of cold borscht, add 1 can condensed vegetarian vegetable soup, ¾ cup sour cream, and blend. Serve chilled.
5. To 1 quart of cold borscht, add 1 can condensed tomato soup, ¾ cup sour cream, and blend. Serve chilled.
6. To 1 quart of cold borscht, add 1 can condensed split pea soup, ¾ cup sour cream, and blend. Serve chilled.

7. To 1 quart of borscht, add 1 can condensed chicken barley soup. Heat and serve hot.
8. To 1 quart of borscht, add 1 can condensed chicken vegetable soup. Heat and serve hot.
9. To 1 quart of borscht, add 1 can condensed lima bean soup. Heat and serve hot with dollops of sour cream.
10. Blend 1 teaspoon grated lemon rind and 1 tablespoon chopped chives into ½ cup sour cream. Serve dollops of sour cream mixture in cold borscht.

HOT BEEF BORSCHT

2 *bunches beets, scraped and sliced*
2 *onions, sliced*
1 *pound flanken or any other soup meat*
2 *quarts water*
1 *large can tomatoes*
Juice of 2 lemons
2 *tablespoons sugar*
1 *teaspoon salt*
¼ *teaspoon pepper*

Put beets and sliced onions in a deep pot. Add soup meat and water. Add tomatoes and rest of ingredients. Bring to boil and simmer for several hours until meat is tender. Puree beets, onions, and tomatoes and return to the soup. Serve hot, with pieces of soup meat in each bowl.
Serves 8.

CHERRY BORSCHT

1 *#2 can sour red pitted cherries*
1 *quart water*
Juice of ½ lemon
3 *tablespoons sugar*
½ *teaspoon salt*
¼ *teaspoon cinnamon*
1 *tablespoon cornstarch*
¼ *cup cold water*
½ *cup sour cream*

Pour cherries with juice into a saucepan and add water, lemon juice, sugar, salt, and cinnamon. Bring to boil and simmer for about 15 minutes or until cherries are very soft. Blend cornstarch with cold water until smooth; add several tablespoons of hot cherry soup and stir until blended. Pour this mixture back into soup, stirring as you pour; continue to stir until thickened. Remove from heat and chill. Blend sour cream into chilled cherry borscht just before serving.
Serves 6.

SCHAV

1 *pound schav (sorrel leaves)* 1 *tablespoon sugar*
1 *quart water* 4 *tablespoons lemon juice*
½ *teaspoon salt* *Sour cream*
1 *onion, diced*

Chop washed sorrel leaves. Place in a saucepan. Add water and salt. Bring to a boil and add onion, sugar, and lemon juice. Simmer for 20 minutes. Chill. Serve with sour cream.
Serves 4.

CABBAGE SOUP

1 *pound soup meat* 1 *medium head cabbage,*
Several beef bones *sliced thin*
2 *quarts water* 1 *potato, peeled and diced*
1 *teaspoon salt* 1 *bay leaf*
2 *onions, sliced* ¼ *cup white seedless raisins*
1 *#2½ can tomatoes* ¼ *cup lemon juice*
1 *can tomato sauce* 2 *tablespoons brown sugar*
  ½ *teaspoon pepper*

Place meat, bones, water, and salt in a large deep pot, and bring to a boil. Skim surface with a large spoon to remove residue.

Turn heat low and add the rest of the ingredients. Simmer for several hours. Taste and add additional lemon juice or sugar as needed to obtain balanced sweet and sour taste desired. *Serves* 8.

CABBAGE BORSCHT

1 *pound soup meat*
Several bones (optional)
2 *quarts water*
1 *2-pound head of cabbage,*
  shredded
5 *beets, scraped and sliced*
  thin

2 *onions, sliced thin*
1 *#202 can tomatoes*
¼ *cup brown sugar*
Juice of 1 *lemon*
1 *teaspoon salt*
¼ *teaspoon ginger*

Simmer meat and bones in water for ½ hour. Meanwhile, put shredded cabbage in a colander, pour boiling water over it, then drain. Skim soup with large spoon, then add cabbage and rest of ingredients. Simmer for 2 hours, covered. Serve with chunks of meat in soup bowls. *Serves* 8.

SAUERKRAUT SOUP

2 *pounds fresh sauerkraut,*
  or 1 *large can*
1 *#2½ can tomatoes*
3 *onions*

2 *pounds beef brisket or*
  flanken
1 *teaspoon salt*
½ *teaspoon pepper*
2 *tablespoons brown sugar*

Combine the sauerkraut and tomatoes in a large pot. Sauté the onions until golden and add to pot. Add beef, salt, pepper, and sugar. Cover with water. Bring to boil, then reduce heat; cover pot and simmer for 3 hours, skimming and stirring occasionally. *Serves* 8.

Almost before it was too late to tell, Mama Laura revealed the secret of why her chicken soup was better than everyone else's. She always added a little sugar to the pot before serving. This small touch enabled her to remain the matriarch of the chicken soup clan until the end of her years. But I am sure she intended the secret to live on, and so I record her recipe here with loving memories.

MAMA LAURA'S CHICKEN SOUP

1 *soup chicken (fowl), about* | 1 *parsnip root, cleaned*
4 *lbs.* | 2 *sprigs parsley*
2 *quarts water* | 2 *sprigs dill*
1 *whole onion, peeled* | 2 *teaspoons salt*
2 *whole carrots, scraped* | ¼ *teaspoon pepper*
4 *stalks celery, including tops* | 2 *teaspoons sugar*

Clean chicken, place in deep pot, add water and remaining ingredients, except sugar. Bring to boil, then simmer covered until chicken is tender, about 2 hours. Remove chicken, strain soup, and chill. Skim off fat which has risen to the top of chilled soup. Reheat soup. Increase seasoning if desired and add sugar. Serve with a piece of soup carrot in each bowl, and with noodles or any other soup accompaniment.
Serves 8.

SPLIT PEA SOUP

2 *cups split peas* | 2 *celery stalks*
1 *pound soup meat* | 1 *teaspoon salt*
2 *quarts water* | ½ *teaspoon sugar*
1 *onion, diced fine* | ⅛ *teaspoon pepper*
2 *whole carrots, scraped* | 2 *frankfurters, sliced*
2 *sprigs parsley, diced fine* | (*optional*)

Rinse, then soak split peas for several hours or overnight. Place in deep pot with soup meat and water. Add remaining ingredients and bring to boil. Simmer, stirring occasionally, for 2 hours, or until meat is tender. Remove meat, skim soup, and rub rest of the ingredients through a sieve or a food mill. Add sliced frankfurters if desired.
Serves 8.

LENTIL SOUP

2 *cups lentils, washed well*
2 *or 3 soup bones*
2 *quarts water*
2 *carrots*
3 *stalks celery*
1 *whole onion, peeled*

1½ *teaspoons salt*
1 *teaspoon sugar*
¼ *teaspoon pepper*
Several sprigs parsley
3 *frankfurters*

Combine all ingredients, except the frankfurters, in a large saucepan and bring to boil. Simmer, stirring occasionally, for about 2 hours, or until lentils are soft. Strain soup, rubbing vegetables through a sieve back into the stock. Add sliced frankfurters and simmer for 10 minutes more.
Serves 8.

LIMA BEAN AND BARLEY SOUP

1 *cup lima beans*
2 *onions, diced*
1 *pound soup meat*
2 *quarts water*
1½ *teaspoons salt*

¼ *teaspoon pepper*
2 *sprigs chopped parsley*
½ *cup barley*
A few mushrooms, dried or
  fresh, sliced

Rinse, then cover lima beans with water and soak overnight. Drain and cook with onions, soup meat, 2 quarts water, salt, pepper, and chopped parsley. Simmer, stirring occasionally, for about 1½ hours, or until beans and meat are tender. Then add barley and mushrooms and simmer for an additional 45 minutes. *Serves* 8.

MUSHROOM-BARLEY SOUP

1 *cup barley*
1 *pound soup meat, or several bones*
2 *quarts water*
1 *onion, diced*
2 *carrots, scraped and diced*
2 *stalks celery, diced fine*

½ *pound fresh mushrooms, sliced*
1 *teaspoon salt*
¼ *teaspoon pepper*
½ *teaspoon sugar*
1 *sprig dill*

Simmer barley and soup meat in the water for 1 hour. Skim surface with a large spoon. Add rest of ingredients and simmer, stirring occasionally, for another hour.
Serves 8.

POTATO SOUP

4 *large potatoes, peeled and diced*
2 *onions, diced*
2 *stalks celery, diced fine*
1 *sprig dill*

2 *cups water*
1 *teaspoon salt*
3 *cups milk*
¼ *cup butter*

Place potatoes, onions, celery, dill, water, and salt in a saucepan; simmer for 20 minutes, or until potatoes are tender. Add milk and butter and stir until heated through.
Serves 4.

POTATO-CHIVE SOUP

4 *large potatoes, peeled*
4 *cups hot milk*
2 *large onions, sliced*
2 *tablespoons butter*
2 *tablespoons flour*
½ *teaspoon salt*

¼ *teaspoon pepper*
1 *tablespoon chopped parsley*
2 *tablespoons chopped chives*
Chopped chives (optional)
Paprika (optional)

Cook the potatoes in a small amount of water until tender. Mash potatoes, including potato water, and add hot milk. Sauté the sliced onions in butter until translucent; quickly blend in flour, and several spoonfuls of the hot potato mixture. Stir onion mixture into the potato and milk mixture. Add salt, pepper, and chopped parsley. Simmer and stir frequently until thick and smooth. Serve hot, topped with a sprinkling of chopped chives and a dash of paprika if desired.
Serves 8.

TOMATO AND RICE SOUP

3 *marrow bones*
2 *quarts water*
2 *#2½ cans tomatoes*
2 *onions, diced fine*
2 *tablespoons sugar*

1 *teaspoon salt*
Juice of 1 lemon
¼ *teaspoon pepper*
½ *teaspoon paprika*
1 *cup cooked rice*

Combine all ingredients except the cooked rice. Simmer for 2 hours, covered. Add rice and reheat just before serving. If thicker soup is desired, mix 2 tablespoons of flour with enough water to make a thin paste; add several spoonfuls of soup to the mixture and then stir it into the soup. Simmer and stir until thickened.
Serves 8.

FISH CHOWDER

2 *potatoes, peeled*
3 *tablespoons butter*
2 *onions, sliced thin*
2 *cups water*

1 *pound fish fillets*
2 *cups milk*
½ *teaspoon salt*
¼ *teaspoon pepper*

Cut potatoes into small cubes. Melt butter in a medium saucepan. Add potatoes, onions, and water, and simmer covered for 15 minutes until vegetables are tender. Cut fish fillets into small chunks and add along with milk, salt, and pepper. Simmer, covered, for an additional 15 or 20 minutes, stirring occasionally. *Serves* 4.

What makes Natalie's vegetable soup superb? Look at the directions and you will see that it is truly a labor of love. Rather than assemble all the ingredients in the pot at the same time, she adds and removes ingredients at intervals in order to get the desired consistency. Sometimes, just before serving she shakes the catsup bottle once or twice into the soup to give it extra flavor.

VEGETABLE SOUP

2 *pounds neck bones, or*
   flanken
2 *quarts water*
2 *onions, whole*
1 *carrot, whole*
1 *teaspoon salt*
½ *teaspoon pepper*
1 *pound lima beans, soaked*
   several hours or overnight

⅓ *cup barley*
1 *can whole tomatoes*
1 *potato, diced*
2 *carrots, diced*
2 *stalks celery, diced*
1 *package cut frozen string*
   beans
1 *package frozen peas*

Place the bones or flanken in a deep pot and cover with water. Bring to boil, then simmer for about 30 minutes, skimming

residue from the top. Add onions, 1 carrot, salt, and pepper, and simmer for 1 hour. Add the soaked lima beans and barley and simmer for another ½ hour, stirring occasionally. Then add the tomatoes, potato, carrots, and celery stalks. Cook another ½ hour. Add string beans and peas and cook for an additional 15 minutes. Remove onions if desired. Add catsup if desired.
Serves 6–8.

CREAM OF CORN SOUP

1 *can whole kernel corn*
1 *can creamed corn*
2 *cups milk*
1 *tablespoon butter*

½ *teaspoon salt*
¼ *teaspoon pepper*
1 *teaspoon sugar*

Combine the cans of corn and milk in a saucepan. Add butter, salt, pepper, and sugar. Heat thoroughly, stirring until butter is melted and blended.
Serves 6.

HOME-TOUCH RANCH CHOWDER

1½ *pounds ground chuck*
½ *teaspoon salt*
¼ *teaspoon pepper*
2 *eggs, slightly beaten*
½ *cup matzo meal*
¼ *cup water*
Fat

1 *can green split pea soup*
1 *can onion soup*
1 *can vegetarian vegetable soup*
3 *soup cans water*
1 *cup uncooked noodles*

Mix meat with salt, pepper, eggs, matzo meal, and ¼ cup water. Form into 30 meat balls. Brown in hot fat in a large saucepan. Drain off fat. Mix the 3 soups and water and add to meat balls.

Stir well; bring to boil, reduce heat, and add noodles. Simmer about 20 minutes, or until meat balls are done.
Serves 6–8.

HOME-TOUCH PEA SOUP

1 *can condensed clear
  chicken soup*
1 *can condensed green split
  pea soup*

1½ *soup cans water*
1 *teaspoon Worcestershire
  sauce*
¾ *cup fine noodles, uncooked*

Combine soups, water, and Worcestershire sauce. Bring to a boil and add noodles. Cover tightly, reduce heat, and simmer for 10 minutes, or until noodles are tender.
Serves 4.

HOME-TOUCH TOMATO SOUP

1 *can tomato soup*
½ *soup can milk*

½ *cup sour cream*
2 *tablespoons chopped chives*

Stir soup and milk until thoroughly blended. Chill and serve with sour cream that has been sprinkled with chopped chives.
Serves 3.

· 6 ·

"The grace of a wife delighteth her husband;
And her discretion will fatten his bones."

JESHU BEN SIRAH

What Goes in the Soup

Soup accompaniments lend variety and interest to the traditional bowls of soup. They are most often served in chicken soup where they contribute a delicious heartiness to an otherwise thin broth. There are many types of packaged noodles, from the thinnest strands to wide lengths, squares, bows, and shells. None, however, can match the unique flavor and texture of homemade noodles, which, as you will see, are not difficult to make.

Noodles, puffs of *mandlen*, stuffed *kreplach*, fluffy balls of *knaidlach*, *farfel*, or barley are wonderful additions to soup. Frequently, the Jewish cook will combine two kinds of soup accompaniments as a surprise offering; for example, fine egg noodles and a ball of *knaidlach* with perhaps half of a soup carrot joining in the swim.

In lentil and bean soups, nothing is as satisfying as a few slices of frankfurter "pennies." A dollop of sour cream and a hot boiled potato are delicious in cold borscht. Rice may be added to chicken soup, pea soup, and tomato soup to give them additional bulk.

In this chapter you will find many tasty garnishes that will add excitement and flavor to your soup course.

HOMEMADE NOODLES

2 *eggs*   ½ *teaspoon salt*
1 *cup flour*

Beat eggs. Mix flour and salt, add to eggs to make a stiff dough. Knead well. Roll into two large thin circles on a large wooden board, and allow dough to dry for about ½ hour. When dry, roll up each circle, jelly-roll style, and slice into thin fine strips. Spread noodles out to dry. To store, place in tightly closed container and keep in dry, cool place. To cook, boil in salted water for 10 minutes, strain, and serve in broth.
Serves 8 as a soup accompaniment.

FARFEL

1 *cup flour*   1 *egg*
½ *teaspoon salt*   2 *cups water or broth*

Mix the flour and salt together. Blend in unbeaten egg until it forms a stiff dough. Roll out pieces of dough into narrow strips about ¼ inch thick and let dry on a cloth. Chop dried dough into fine pieces about the size of barley, and spread them out to dry further. To store, place in a tightly closed container and keep in a dry cool place. To cook, boil in water or broth for 10 minutes; drain and serve in soup.
Serves 8.

MATZO FARFEL

2 *slices matzo*   2 *tablespoons chicken fat*
2 *eggs, beaten*   ¼ *teaspoon salt*

Crush matzo into fine crumbs. Add beaten eggs. Heat chicken fat in a skillet; add crumb mixture and stir constantly while cooking, breaking the mixture into small particles. Let stand for several hours until dry. Add to hot soup when serving.
Serves 8.

Every balabusta *has her own particular way of making* knaidlach *according to the accustomed taste or heritage of her family. Some like a* knaidle *(singular) to be light and fluffy, others prefer it firm or even hard. Some insist that it should zing with pepper, others consider the addition of chopped parsley an abomination, and there are even cooks who advocate the use of seltzer (carbonated water) instead of plain water. The trick to getting your favorite kind of* knaidlach *perfectly round is to rub your hands with chicken fat before forming the balls.*

KNAIDLACH

2 *tablespoons chicken fat*   ⅛ *teaspoon pepper*
¾ *cup water*   1 *egg, unbeaten*
1 *cup matzo meal*   2 *quarts water or broth*
1 *teaspoon salt*

Melt the fat in a saucepan containing ¾ cup boiling water. Add the matzo meal, salt, and pepper, and stir over medium heat until the dough forms a ball and leaves the sides of the pan. Remove the mixture from the heat. Add the egg, beating until a smooth, thick dough is formed. Cover the pan and chill for 1 hour. Shape dough into 1-inch balls. Drop the balls into 2 quarts of boiling water or broth. Cook for 20 minutes. The *knaidlach* will double in size during cooking. Serve in hot chicken soup. *Makes about 12 large fluffy* knaidlach.

MATZO DUMPLINGS

2 *tablespoons cold water*	½ *teaspoon salt*
2 *eggs, well beaten*	1 *tablespoon chopped parsley*
½ *cup matzo meal*	*Pinch of nutmeg*
½ *teaspoon baking powder*	1 *quart water*

Add cold water to beaten eggs. Add matzo meal, baking powder, salt, and chopped parsley. Add a pinch of nutmeg. With moist hands, form into 1-inch balls. Drop the dumplings into a quart of boiling water. Cover and cook in rapidly boiling water over medium heat for about 30 minutes. Remove with a slotted spoon when cooked through. Serve in soup or as a side dish. *Makes 1 dozen.*

EGG DUMPLINGS

1 *egg*	½ *teaspoon salt*
½ *cup water*	1½ *cups flour*

Beat egg until lemon-colored. Add water and salt. Stir in flour to form a smooth batter. Drop by teaspoonfuls into rapidly boiling broth or water. Cover and cook over medium heat for about

30 minutes. If dumplings seem tough, add a little more water to the batter. Serve in soup or in stews.
Serves 4.

Kreplach can be half-round, triangular, or rectangular. They are usually boiled in salted water and served in a bowl of Mama's chicken soup, but they can also be parboiled, then fried in hot fat until browned, and served as a side dish at lunch or dinner. Once they are boiled they can be refrigerated in a covered container for several days, and reheated in the soup or fried.

KREPLACH

Dough:

2 *eggs*

1 *teaspoon salt*

¼ *cup water*

1 *cup flour*

Filling:

½ *pound cooked soup meat*

1 *small onion*

1 *egg, beaten*

1 *tablespoon chicken fat*

½ *teaspoon salt*

⅛ *teaspoon pepper*

To make dough: Beat eggs lightly; add salt and water. Add flour gradually, using just enough to make a soft dough. If dough seems too dry, add a little more water. Knead gently, then rest dough on a floured board and cover with a large warm bowl. After ½ hour, roll out dough on a floured board until very thin, and cut into 2-inch circles or squares. Fill with meat filling using 1 teaspoon per *kreplach* and fold in half, pinching to seal the edges around filling.

To make filling: Grind the meat and onion together very fine. Add the egg, chicken fat, salt, and pepper.

Dry filled *kreplach* on clean kitchen towels for about 1 hour. Then drop in boiling salted water and cook for about 15

minutes. Remove with a slotted spoon and reheat in chicken soup just before serving.
Makes about 2 dozen.

MANDLEN

3 *tablespoons chicken fat*   ¾ *cup matzo meal*
¼ *cup water*   2 *eggs, unbeaten*
½ *teaspoon salt*

In a small saucepan, heat fat, water, and salt to the boiling point. Mix matzo meal in quickly, stirring until smooth. Beat in eggs, blending well. Rub hands with a thin coating of fat; shape mixture into ¼-inch balls. Place on a greased cookie sheet and bake at 400 degrees for about 30 minutes, or until golden brown. Serve in hot soup.
Makes about 8 dozen.

· 7 ·

"Strength and dignity are her clothing;
And she laugheth at the time to come."

BOOK OF PROVERBS

Cooking the Catch

In a traditional Jewish home, fish may be served as the main course in a dairy meal and prepared with *milchig* ingredients, or it may be served as the appetizer course in a *fleishig* meal and prepared with *pareve* ingredients. Whatever its purpose, the fish course is bound to be a tasty offering.

Low in calories and fat, fish is an important part of Jewish cookery. Most of the recipes use fresh water fish, the type that was available from local streams in the inland countries where Jewish fish cookery originated. There is a variety of interesting ways to prepare fish. It can be pickled, stuffed and baked, fried, simmered, barbecued, prepared sweet and sour, or served in balls as gefilte fish.

Arguments over the best way to prepare gefilte fish are to be expected whenever two or more *balabustas* compare recipes. It is a source of great pride to be able to prepare this treasured dish well. However, some cooks like it sweet, others like it peppery; some like to shape the fish into large, oval-shaped balls, some make the balls small and round, and some people insist that the fish should be stuffed back into the whole fish skin and poached in a loaf. Everyone agrees, however, that a serving of red or white horseradish adds a zesty flavor to gefilte fish.

In Jewish homes herring is often served for breakfast, with gobs of sour cream and onions. It can also be baked in wine sauce, prepared sweet and sour, barbecued over hot coals, or chopped with apples into a spicy salad. Haddock, halibut, and whitefish are often just smothered with vegetables and seasonings and baked.

No matter what your preference, cooking fish properly is an art. The recipes in this chapter will enhance your ability to prepare savory fish dishes which will long be remembered.

Of all the gefilte fish recipes I tested, I liked Aunt Gert's the best. She notes that some fish contains less water than others, so that it may be necessary to add water, a little at a time, if the consistency seems too hard when you chop the fish. If you put the chopper in the middle of the fish mixture, and the chopper stands upright, you probably have the right amount of liquid.

GEFILTE FISH

4 *pounds whitefish, filleted*
2 *pounds pike, filleted*
3 *onions, diced*
3 *eggs, slightly beaten*
⅓ *cup matzo meal ·*
¼ *cup ice water*
1 *tablespoon salt*
½ *teaspoon pepper*
2 *tablespoons sugar*

3 *onions*
3 *large carrots, scraped and sliced*
Heads, bones, and skin of fish
3 *sprigs parsley*
1 *quart water*
1 *tablespoon salt*
1 *tablespoon sugar*

Place whole onions, carrots, fish heads, bones and skin, and parsley in a large deep pot. Add 1 quart water, 1 tablespoon salt, 1 tablespoon sugar and bring to a boil. Reduce heat. Meanwhile, grind fish and onions, or chop fine. Add eggs, matzo meal, and water. Add salt, pepper, and sugar. Form fish mixture into oval-shaped balls using about ½ cup of fish mixture for each ball. Drop carefully into the simmering fish stock. Cover and simmer for 2 hours. Cool. Remove from broth with a slotted spoon. Strain broth and pour over fish balls. Chill. Broth will jell as it cools. Serve a little jellied broth and a carrot slice or two with each portion. Pass the dish of horseradish.
Makes 12–14 pieces.

HOME-TOUCH GEFILTE FISH

1 *large jar gefilte fish*

2 *Bermuda onions, sliced*

Empty large jar of gefilte fish with juice into a medium-size saucepan. Add onion slices and simmer until they are soft. Refrigerate until serving time.
Serves 8.

BAKED BLUEFISH

1 bouillon cube
⅓ cup hot water
½ pound mushrooms, cut up
3 stalks celery, diced
1 green pepper, diced
2 onions, diced

1 large whole bluefish, about
   4 pounds, cleaned and split
1 1-pound can whole green
   asparagus
1 teaspoon paprika
1 cup tomato juice

In a skillet, dissolve the bouillon cube in hot water. Add the mushrooms, celery, pepper, and onions and simmer until well cooked. Stuff into the bluefish and place into a suitable greased roasting pan. Place asparagus on top of stuffing and hold together with toothpicks. Sprinkle paprika over top of fish. Pour tomato juice over all. Bake at 350 degrees for 25 minutes.
Serves 4.

STUFFED BAKED FISH

1 large whole haddock, about
   4 pounds, cleaned and split
2 cups day-old bread,
   shredded
1 tablespoon chopped onion
1 tablespoon chopped celery
   leaves

1 teaspoon dried tarragon
1 teaspoon dill seeds
1 teaspoon poultry seasoning
½ cup tomato juice
½ teaspoon salt
¼ teaspoon pepper
2 tablespoons butter

Wash and dry fish. Place bread in bowl; add onion, celery leaves, and seasonings. Moisten with tomato juice. Stuff fish with mixture and place in shallow baking dish. Dot top of stuffing with butter. Bake at 375 degrees for about 30 minutes.
Serves 4.

BAKED FISH AND VEGETABLES

1 *pound of haddock, filleted*
½ *teaspoon salt*
¼ *teaspoon pepper*
2 *tablespoons butter*
1 *onion, diced*

1 *green pepper, seeded and diced*
1 *1-pound can whole tomatoes*
½ *teaspoon sugar*
Bay leaf

Arrange fillets in a flat greased baking dish. Sprinkle with salt and pepper. Dot with butter. Scatter the onion and pepper around the fillets. Empty the can of tomatoes, spooning evenly over all. Sprinkle the sugar over the tomatoes. Break a bay leaf in half and tuck into the tomatoes, remembering to remove it before serving. Bake for 25 minutes at 350 degrees.
Serves 2–3.

HADDOCK-WINE CASSEROLE

2½ *pounds haddock fillets*
5 *tablespoons melted butter*
Juice of ½ lemon
⅔ *cup dry white wine*
1 *onion, sliced*
1 *green pepper, chopped fine*

1 *carrot, scraped and cut in thin slices*
2 *tablespoons flour*
¼ *cup heavy cream*
3 *egg yolks, beaten*
¼ *teaspoon salt*
⅛ *teaspoon pepper*

Place fish in buttered casserole. Sprinkle with 2 tablespoons of butter, the lemon juice, and half the wine. Arrange onion slices, chopped pepper, and carrot slices evenly over fish. Bake, covered, in 375-degree oven for 20 minutes. Pour off liquid stock and reserve. Melt 3 tablespoons butter in top of double boiler; stir in flour; add cream, egg yolks, remaining wine, and fish stock. Heat mixture slowly over hot water, stirring constantly until thick. Add salt and pepper. Serve sauce over fish.
Serves 6.

BAKED HALIBUT WITH CUCUMBER SAUCE

3 *halibut steaks, each 1 inch*
  thick
½ *cup chopped onion*
1 *tablespoon minced parsley*
1 *teaspoon salt*

⅛ *teaspoon pepper*
1 *egg yolk*
2 *tablespoons lemon juice*
3 *tablespoons melted butter*

Place halibut steaks in a greased roasting pan. Sprinkle with onion, parsley, salt, and pepper. Combine the egg yolk, lemon juice, and melted butter. Pour over tops of halibut steaks. Bake for 30 minutes at 375 degrees.

Cucumber Sauce:
2 *large cucumbers, grated*
1 *small onion, grated*
1 *teaspoon tarragon vinegar*

1 *teaspoon salt*
3 *tablespoons heavy sweet*
  cream

Combine cucumbers, onion, vinegar, salt, and cream in top of double boiler. Heat over boiling water, stirring occasionally, while fish is baking.
Serves 3.

EPICUREAN FISH CASSEROLE

¼ *cup butter or margarine*
1 *medium onion, chopped*
3 *tablespoons flour*
1 *teaspoon salt*
⅛ *teaspoon pepper*
2½ *cups milk*
1 *12-ounce package frozen*
  lima beans, partially cooked

1 *1-pound jar gefilte fish,*
  drained and mashed
1 *cup grated cheese: Parmesan,*
  swiss, or cheddar
1 *cup crackers, coarsely*
  broken
1 *large tomato, sliced*

Sauté onion in butter or margarine until tender; blend in flour, salt, and pepper. Stirring constantly, gradually blend in milk and

cook over low heat until sauce is smooth and thickened. Remove from heat. In a greased 1½-quart baking dish, arrange alternate layers of lima beans, gefilte fish, ¾ cup of the cheese, cracker bits, and sauce. Top with tomato slices and sprinkle with remaining ¼ cup cheese. Bake in a 350-degree over for 30 minutes, or until tomato is tender and cheese golden brown.
Serves 4.

This recipe for Sweet and Sour Fish is an heirloom from my maternal grandmother. It was given to me with up-to-date directions by my dependable Aunt Ceil, who suggests that as much as five pounds of fish can be cooked with the same seasonings with great success.

SWEET AND SOUR FISH

2 *large onions, sliced*
¾ *cup vinegar*
¾ *cup sugar*
1 *teaspoon salt*

½ *teaspoon pepper*
1 *teaspoon powdered ginger*
3 *pounds whitefish, pike, or*
  salmon steak

Place sliced onions in the bottom of a large saucepan or Dutch oven, and cover with water. Simmer onions for 10 minutes. Add vinegar, sugar, salt, pepper, and ginger and simmer for 5 minutes more. Turn flame off, add fish to pot, and marinate for about 10 minutes before cooking; if necessary, add more water until fish is covered. Simmer fish for 45 minutes in the covered pot, testing occasionally for doneness and to see whether it is necessary to add more water to keep fish covered.

Note: When buying fish, have fish man remove the innards and slice fish into desired number of pieces, each 2 to 3 inches thick. Have him leave skin on and bones intact to insure that fish holds together during cooking.
Serves 6.

SWEET AND SOUR PICKLED FISH

Fish heads
3 onions, sliced
3 pounds fresh whitefish, cut
   in 2-inch pieces
2 cups vinegar

½ cup sugar
1 tablespoon pickling spices
½ teaspoon cinnamon
2 lemons, sliced thin

Have fish man give you several fish heads along with the white-fish. Place the fish heads and half of the onions in the bottom of a deep saucepan; add enough water to cover and simmer for 20 minutes. Remove fish heads and discard. Place pieces of whitefish in stock. Add vinegar, sugar, pickling spices, and cinnamon. Add additional water if necessary to cover fish. Simmer for 20 minutes more. Remove pieces of fish care-fully; strain stock; arrange fish in a container, layering remaining onion slices and slices of lemon between layers of fish. Pour strained stock over all. Broth will jell as it cools. Cover and refrigerate for 2 days. Serve with jellied broth.
Serves 6.

SPICED CARP

3 pounds fresh carp
Salt
2 bay leaves
¼ teaspoon black pepper
1 teaspoon cloves

1 tablespoon vinegar
1 lemon, sliced
1 can anchovies
2 egg yolks

Salt carp and let stand several hours, then wash it. Place in heavy skillet with bay leaves, black pepper, cloves, and vinegar. Add water to cover. Add lemon slices and anchovies. Simmer until carp is tender but holds together. Remove fish to warm platter. Strain fish broth and return to skillet. Beat egg yolks, slowly add

some hot broth to the beaten yolks, thinning and beating for several minutes. Then stir yolk mixture quickly into remaining broth in skillet, keeping heat turned low and stirring until slightly thickened. Serve thickened broth as sauce for fish.
Serves 6–8.

PICKLED SALMON

2½ *cups water*
1 *cup vinegar*
4 *onions, sliced*
2 *teaspoons salt*

2 *tablespoons sugar*
1 *tablespoon pickling spices*
2 *pounds fresh salmon steaks, cubed*

In a medium saucepan, boil water, vinegar, and half the onions for 15 minutes. Add salt, sugar, pickling spices, and salmon. Simmer for about 10 minutes, or until salmon is tender. Remove fish with a slotted spoon and store it in the refrigerator with the remaining onion slices layered between the salmon chunks. Pour cooking liquid (unstrained) over fish and cover tightly.
Serves 4.

POACHED SALMON WITH LEMON SAUCE

1 *carrot, sliced*
1 *onion, sliced thin*
1 *bay leaf*
2 *cloves*
½ *teaspoon salt*

¼ *teaspoon pepper*
2 *pounds fresh salmon steaks*
1 *teaspoon sugar*
1 *egg*
2 *tablespoons lemon juice*

Place carrot, onion, bay leaf, cloves, salt, and pepper in a skillet. Arrange salmon steaks on top. Cover with water and simmer gently for 20 minutes, or until fish is tender but the slices remain whole. With a wire whisk, briskly beat the sugar and egg together. Add the lemon juice and 3 tablespoons of the stock

from the simmering fish. This forms a lemon sauce to be served over the fish slices.
Serves 4.

POTATO-SALMON PANCAKES

1 *8-ounce can salmon*
1 *onion, grated*
2 *raw potatoes, grated*
1 *raw carrot, grated*
1 *egg, beaten*

2 *tablespoons breadcrumbs or*
  matzo meal
½ *teaspoon salt*
⅛ *teaspoon pepper*
1 *cup peanut oil*

Flake salmon. Blend with onion, potatoes, and carrot. Add egg. Add breadcrumbs, salt, and pepper. Heat peanut oil in a large skillet. Using a large serving spoon, drop salmon mixture into the hot fat. Fry until browned on one side, turn with a spatula and fry until brown on the other side. Drain on paper toweling to remove excess fat.
Serves 4.

BAKED FISH LOAF

1 *cup milk, boiled*
2 *slices stale bread*
¾ *pound pike, skinned and*
  boned
½ *teaspoon salt*

¼ *teaspoon pepper*
4 *egg yolks, beaten*
½ *glass cream*
4 *egg whites, stiffly beaten*

Combine milk and bread and cook and stir until mixture leaves the side of the saucepan. Cool. Put pike in a blender and blend very fine, or grind it. Scrape fish into a bowl, add salt, pepper, egg yolks, and bread mixture. Add cream. Fold in egg whites. Put into a greased 1-quart casserole and bake 45 minutes at 350 degrees.
Serves 4.

HOT FISH MOUSSE

2 *pounds halibut fillets*
1½ *pounds fresh salmon*
fillets
4 *eggs, separated*
1 *pint sweet cream*

6 *tablespoons melted butter*
½ *teaspoon salt*
¼ *teaspoon pepper*
1 *tablespoon chopped parsley*
Butter

Grind each fish separately. Beat egg whites until stiff. Combine yolks, sweet cream, melted butter, salt, pepper, and parsley; fold into beaten egg whites. Divide batter in half; fold ground halibut into one half and ground salmon into the other half.

Butter a 2-quart mold. Place salmon mixture in bottom of mold and halibut mixture on top. Set mold in a pan of water and bake in 350-degree oven for 1 hour. Turn out on platter and serve hot. *Serves* 8.

SWEET AND SOUR HERRING

2 *miltz herrings*
1 *onion, sliced*
2 *teaspoons sugar*
½ *teaspoon sour salt*

¼ *teaspoon pepper*
1 *teaspoon ginger*
2 *cups water*

Soak herrings overnight; clean. In a saucepan, combine the sliced onion, sugar, sour salt, pepper, ginger, and water. Boil for 15 minutes, then add herrings and simmer an additional 15 to 20 minutes. Slice and serve.
Serves 2–4.

BARBECUED HERRING

2 *large whole miltz herrings,*
gutted, but unwashed and
unskinned

1 *cup flour*

Roll herrings in flour. Wrap each herring in five large sheets of newspaper, each tightly closed. Place on a rack over hot coals. The flour protects the herring from burning as the paper chars away. Roast for about five minutes. Peel off charred paper and flour casing, and serve hot.
Serves 4.

· 8 ·

"Better a dinner of herbs, where love is,
Than a stalled ox, and hatred therewith."

BOOK OF PROVERBS

Meaty with Memories

The koshering of meat is one of the most important events in a traditional Jewish kitchen. After purchasing meat which conforms to the Jewish dietary standards, the housewife further rids the meat of blood. It is soaked in cold water for half an hour, rinsed, salted with coarse salt, and drained on a slanted board for at least an hour. After being rinsed thoroughly again, it is ready to be roasted or braised. If the meat is to be broiled, the home koshering process can be eliminated. A simple salting is enough for broiled meat and liver.

Beef, veal, and lamb are the most popular meats. Kosher rules state that only the forequarters of animals may be used, and since this section does not provide the tenderest cuts of meat many of the meat dishes are potted or roasted and served with superbly seasoned gravies. Ground meat dishes are also praiseworthy, with stuffed cabbage in the fore.

It is interesting to note that many American dishes have been adapted to Kosher regulations and assimilated into the ancient traditions of Jewish cooking. It is not unusual to be served barbecued lamb riblets, glazed corned beef, or boned shoulder of veal roast in a Jewish home. Within her dietary limitations, the Jewish cook has created interesting and delicious meat dishes which are well worth your efforts to reproduce.

BRISKET POT ROAST

4 or 5-pound brisket of beef
2 onions, sliced thin
1 teaspoon salt
½ teaspoon pepper

2 bay leaves
1 cup water
1 teaspoon paprika
6 parboiled potatoes

Place brisket in a Dutch oven. Spread onions around meat. Sprinkle with salt and pepper. Place bay leaves in pot. Add water around sides. Sprinkle with paprika. Cover and roast in a slow (325-degree) oven for 3 hours. Add parboiled potatoes to the gravy, coating well. Roast uncovered an additional hour to finish potatoes and brown roast. Serve in thick slices.
Serves 6.

SAUERBRATEN

4-*pound beef roast or brisket*
of beef
2 *cups vinegar*
1 *cup water*
1 *tablespoon sugar*
3 *whole cloves*
2 *bay leaves*
6 *whole peppercorns*
2 *onions, sliced*
½ *cup flour*
½ *cup oil*
1 *onion, sliced (optional)*
8 *gingersnaps*

Heat vinegar, water, sugar, cloves, bay leaves, peppercorns, and onions for 10 minutes. Cool. Place meat in a large deep bowl and cover with cooled marinade. Refrigerate for 2 days, turning meat morning and night. Remove meat from marinade and wipe dry. Pat with flour. Brown in oil on all sides. Place in a Dutch oven and add 1 cup of the marinade and an additional sliced onion if desired. Simmer, covered, until meat is tender. Remove meat and crumble gingersnaps into the gravy; boil gravy until it thickens, then serve on sliced beef.
Serves 8.

SWEET AND SOUR BRISKET

4-*pound brisket of beef*
1 *pound sauerkraut, canned*
or fresh
2 *small cans tomato sauce*
3 *apples, peeled and sliced*
2 *onions, sliced*
2 *tablespoons brown sugar*
Juice of 2 lemons
½ *teaspoon salt*
¼ *teaspoon pepper*

Arrange brisket in a large Dutch oven. Combine remaining ingredients and pour around the brisket. Cover and simmer for about 2½-3 hours, adding water if necessary to keep brisket from sticking. Adjust sweet and sour taste of the gravy by adding more lemon juice (or vinegar) or sugar until desired taste is achieved. Serve slices with gravy.
Serves 8.

BRISKET ARCADIA

6-*pound brisket of beef*
2 *teaspoons salt*
1 *teaspoon pepper*
5 *white potatoes, peeled and*
halved

2 *pounds extra-large prunes*
1 *cup dark corn syrup*
4 *sweet potatoes, peeled and*
halved

Season meat with salt and pepper; place flat in a large Dutch oven. Cover with water about 3 inches above the meat and simmer covered for 30 minutes. Add halved white potatoes, prunes, and corn syrup. Again, bring to a boil and simmer covered for about 3 hours. Skim fat if desired. Add sweet potatoes, cover, and simmer for 2 more hours until meat is tender. Be certain that meat is always covered with liquid, adding more water if necessary. Do not stir, but shake the pot from side to side to be certain that meat is not sticking. Serve sliced meat surrounded with prunes and potatoes.
Serves 8.

MEAT TZIMMES

3-*pound brisket of beef,*
first cut
6 *white potatoes, peeled and*
quartered
3 *large yams, peeled and*
quartered

18 *large sour prunes*
1 *bay leaf*
1 *teaspoon salt*
½ *teaspoon pepper*
1 *teaspoon sugar*

Trim excess fat from beef. In a large Dutch oven, place half the white potatoes, half the yams, and half the sour prunes. Tuck the bay leaf into the middle. Place meat over this and cover with the remaining potatoes and prunes. Sprinkle with salt, pepper, and sugar. Cover with water and bring to a boil; then turn heat down and simmer tightly covered for about 2½ hours.
Serves 6.

Religious Jewish people will not light the oven or stove during the Sabbath, although it is permissible to keep a dish warm over a previously lit fire. One of the favorite Sabbath dishes in tradition-observing Jewish homes is cholent, since its flavor is not impaired by long, slow cooking. It is put into the oven before sundown on Friday night and baked at low heat until serving time on Saturday. Cholent was once composed solely of beans, but modern recipes, such as the following one, include meat.

CHOLENT

3-pound brisket of beef	1 cup uncooked barley
2 large onions, sliced	1 teaspoon salt
1 clove garlic, minced	½ teaspoon pepper
3 tablespoons chicken fat or cooking oil	1 teaspoon paprika
	½ teaspoon ginger
1 cup dried lima beans, soaked overnight	1 bay leaf
	Boiling water

Brown brisket, onions, and garlic in the fat or oil in a heavy Dutch oven. Add lima beans and barley around the brisket. Season with salt, pepper, paprika, and ginger. Place the bay leaf in the pot. Add boiling water to cover all. Cover with a tight lid, and bake overnight in a 250-degree oven. Or, if desired, you may bake cholent for 6 or 7 hours.
Serves 6.

GLAZED CORNED BEEF

4- to 5-pound corned beef	½ teaspoon rosemary
3 onions, sliced	1 stalk celery
1 bay leaf	12 whole cloves
1 clove garlic	

Sauce:

2 *tablespoons margarine* 3 *tablespoons vinegar*
5 *tablespoons catsup* ⅓ *cup brown sugar*
1 *tablespoon prepared mustard*

Cover meat with water and add onions, bay leaf, garlic clove, rosemary, and celery. Bring to a boil, then simmer slowly about 4 hours, or until tender. While corned beef is simmering combine the ingredients for the sauce. Drain cooked corned beef and place in a roasting pan. Dot with cloves. Pour sauce over corned beef. Roast in a 350-degree over for 30 minutes, basting frequently to brown.
Serves 8–10.

BEEF GOULASH

2 *onions, sliced* 1 *teaspoon salt*
1 *clove garlic, diced* ¼ *teaspoon pepper*
2 *tablespoons chicken fat* 1 *teaspoon paprika*
2 *pounds beef, cubed* 5 *potatoes, peeled and*
½ *cup tomato puree* *quartered*
1 *bay leaf*

Brown onions and garlic in the chicken fat in Dutch oven. Add beef cubes and sear on all sides, turning frequently to prevent burning. Lower heat, add tomato puree, and bay leaf. Season with salt, pepper, and paprika. Cover and simmer, adding water if gravy becomes too thick. After 1 hour, add potatoes and cook for an additional 30 minutes, or until potatoes are soft. Remove bay leaf and serve goulash with gravy.
Serves 6.

STEAK ROLL-UPS

3 *pounds shoulder steak, cut*
  ¼ inch thick
1 *onion, minced*
2 *tablespoons shortening or*
  chicken fat
3 *matzos, coarsely broken*
¼ *teaspoon pepper*

1 *teaspoon salt*
6 *tablespoons hot water*
½ *cup matzo meal*
Fat
1 *can tomato and mushroom*
  sauce
¼ *cup water*

Cut meat into 6 or 8 portions and pound very thin. Sauté onion in fat. Combine with broken matzos, pepper, salt, and hot water. Place a spoonful of stuffing in the center of each piece of meat. Roll up and fasten with toothpicks, skewers, or string. Roll in the matzo meal. Brown in a small amount of fat in the skillet. Add tomato and mushroom sauce and water; cover, and simmer about 1 hour, or until tender.
Serves 6–8.

STUFFED CABBAGE

1 *large leafy head cabbage*
2 *pounds lean ground beef*
1 *onion, grated*
1 *apple, grated*
1 *cup water*
1 *cup Minute Rice*
½ *teaspoon salt*
¼ *teaspoon pepper*
1 *#2½ can of tomatoes*

1 *cup brown sugar*
2 *tablespoons vinegar*
Juice of 1 *lemon*
1 *onion, sliced*
1 *cup seedless raisins*
  (optional)
5 *gingersnaps, crumbled*
½ *teaspoon salt*

Parboil cabbage. Cut around the core, and carefully remove leaves one by one. Trim heavy center lines where necessary. Combine ground beef, grated onion, grated apple, water, rice, salt, and pepper. Place about 2 tablespoons of meat mixture in center near bottom of each cabbage leaf; fold bottom up, fold in each side, and roll up. Cut up extra cabbage leaves and place

in bottom of a deep pot. Add tomatoes, brown sugar, vinegar, lemon juice, onion slices, raisins, gingersnaps, and salt. Place rolled cabbage leaves, open side down, into the pot. Simmer covered for 2 hours.
Serves 6–8.

STUFFED CABBAGE WITH SAUERKRAUT

1 *large leafy head cabbage*
2 *pounds lean ground beef*
1 *onion, grated*
1 *cup Minute Rice*
1 *teaspoon salt*
¼ *teaspoon pepper*

1 *cup water*
2 *cups tomato juice*
1 *large can sauerkraut*
½ *cup brown sugar*
Juice of 2 lemons
1 *onion, sliced*

Parboil cabbage. Cut around the core, and carefully remove leaves one by one. Trim heavy center lines where necessary. Combine ground beef, grated onion, rice, salt, pepper, and water. Place about 2 tablespoons of meat mixture in center near bottom of each cabbage leaf; fold bottom up, fold in each side, and roll up. Cut up extra cabbage leaves and place in bottom of a deep pot. Add tomato juice, sauerkraut, brown sugar, lemon juice, and sliced onion. Place rolled cabbage leaves, open side down, into the pot. Simmer covered for 2 hours.
Serves 6–8.

SWEET AND SOUR MEAT BALLS

2 *pounds lean ground beef*
1 *egg*
¼ *cup grated bread crumbs*
1 *onion, grated*
¼ *teaspoon garlic powder*
1 *teaspoon salt*
½ *teaspoon pepper*
2 *tablespoons chopped parsley*

½ *cup cold water*
½ *cup oil*
1 *#2½ can whole tomatoes*
1 *small can tomato sauce*
Juice of 1 lemon
2 *tablespoons brown sugar*
6 *gingersnaps, crumbled*

In a large bowl, combine the chopped meat, egg, bread crumbs, and grated onion. Add garlic powder, salt, pepper, and chopped parsley. Work in the cold water. Form tiny meat balls and sauté in hot oil in large skillet, turning carefully to brown on all sides. Pour off remaining oil. Combine tomatoes, tomato sauce, lemon juice, brown sugar, and crushed gingersnaps. Pour over meat balls, cover tightly, and simmer for 1 hour.
Serves 6.

MEAT LOAF WITH HARD-COOKED EGG CENTER

2 *pounds lean ground beef*	2 *tablespoons chopped parsley*
3 *slices white bread, soaked*	1 *teaspoon salt*
in ½ *cup water*	½ *teaspoon pepper*
2 *eggs, slightly beaten*	½ *teaspoon garlic powder*
¼ *cup water*	6 *hard-cooked eggs, shelled*
1 *large onion, grated*	1 *small can tomato sauce*

Combine ground beef and soaked white bread, mixing gently. Add beaten eggs and water. Add grated onion, parsley, salt, pepper, and garlic powder. Put half of the meat mixture in a greased pan 12 by 4 inches; line up the hard-cooked eggs end-to-end down the middle of the loaf pan; top with the remaining meat mixture. Pour tomato sauce over the top. Bake at 350 degrees for 1 hour. Cut in thick slices so that the egg remains in the center of each slice.
Serves 6.

MATZO MEAT LOAF

2 *pounds lean ground beef*	¾ *cup matzo meal*
1 *teaspoon salt*	¼ *cup tomato juice*
¼ *teaspoon pepper*	¼ *cup catsup*
2 *eggs, slightly beaten*	½ *cup finely minced onion*

Season beef with salt and pepper. Add eggs and matzo meal. Add tomato juice, catsup, and minced onion. Form into a rectangular loaf, 1 inch thick, in a shallow pan. Place 4 to 5 inches away from the flame unit and broil for 10 to 15 minutes without turning.
Serves 6–8.

STUFFED PEPPERS

8 *large green peppers*
1 *pound ground lean beef*
½ *cup cooked rice*
1 *egg*
1 *small onion, grated*
¼ *cup tomato puree*

½ *teaspoon salt*
¼ *teaspoon pepper*
1 *#2½ can whole tomatoes*
Juice of 1 lemon
2 *tablespoons brown sugar*
¼ *cup seedless raisins*

Wash green peppers and cut in half lengthwise. Remove seeds and membranes. Combine ground beef, cooked rice, egg, grated onion, and tomato puree. Season with salt and pepper. Stuff halves of peppers with this mixture. In a Dutch oven, combine the tomatoes with the lemon juice, brown sugar, and raisins. Place stuffed peppers in this sauce. Cover tightly and bake in a 350-degree oven for 40 minutes.
Serves 8.

Kosher steaks are notoriously tough, since the meat comes from the animal's forequarter. However, if you select the meat carefully, you will be able to serve a good steak dinner. Choose either the first cuts of the rib with the bone in, or the eye of the rib, making sure that the meat is well marbled with fat. Have it cut ¾ inch thick for quick grilling. Do use a tenderizer if you have any doubts about the meat's fat distribution.

BROILED RIB STEAK

4 ¾-inch-thick rib steaks   1 clove garlic, minced
Meat tenderizer   Salt

Arrange the steaks on a broiling pan. Sprinkle with meat tenderizer and let stand at room temperature for 1 hour. Rub with minced garlic, and sprinkle lightly with salt. Broil for 7 minutes on each side, or longer to achieve desired degree of doneness. *Serves 4–6.*

RIB ROAST

2 or 3 ribs of beef   1 teaspoon salt
1 teaspoon paprika   2 onions, sliced
1 clove garlic, crushed

Place roast beef in a large roasting pan. Combine paprika, crushed garlic, and salt and rub over the roast. Place slices of onion around the roast. Add ½ inch of water to the bottom of the pan. Roast in a 350-degree oven for about 20 minutes to the pound, or use a meat thermometer for best results. *Serves 6–8.*

VEAL POT ROAST

3-pound shoulder of veal,   ½ teaspoon salt
   boned and tied   ¼ teaspoon pepper
1 clove garlic, peeled and   Oil
   mashed   1 onion, sliced
1 tablespoon paprika   1 cup water

Rub meat with mashed garlic. Season with paprika, salt, and pepper. Brown on all sides in hot oil in a Dutch oven. Add sliced onion and water to browned roast. Cover and simmer for 1 hour,

adding more water if necessary to keep from sticking. Serve sliced hot or cold.
Serves 6.

VEAL ROAST WITH SAUERKRAUT

3-*pound shoulder of veal,*
  boned and tied
2 *onions, sliced thin*
1 *clove garlic, minced*
2 *tablespoons chicken fat*

2 *teaspoons salt*
3 *teaspoons paprika*
1 *1-pound can sauerkraut,*
  juice included
1 *teaspoon caraway seeds*

Season veal roast with salt and pepper and set aside. In a Dutch oven, sauté onions and garlic in chicken fat. Add salt and paprika. Add sauerkraut and caraway seeds; stir. Place veal roast in the center of Dutch oven, cover, and simmer for about 2 hours, or until tender. Slice and serve with sauerkraut gravy.
Serves 6.

VEAL ROLLS SAUTERNE

2 *pounds ground veal*
½ *cup matzo meal*
2 *eggs, slightly beaten*
¼ *cup water*
¼ *cup minced parsley*
1 *teaspoon salt*

½ *teaspoon ginger*
Matzo meal
½ *cup fat*
1 *can condensed clear*
  chicken soup
¾ *cup sauterne*

Combine veal, matzo meal, eggs, water, minced parsley, salt, and ginger. Shape into 12 rolls about 3 inches long. Roll in matzo meal. Brown in fat. Blend soup and wine; pour over meat. Cover and bring to a boil. Reduce heat and simmer covered about 30 minutes.
Serves 6.

STUFFED BREAST OF VEAL

1 *large breast of veal*
2 *onions, diced*
2 *tablespoons chicken fat*
2 *cups coarse bread crumbs*
2 *apples, diced*

½ *teaspoon salt*
¼ *teaspoon pepper*
½ *teaspoon rosemary*
1 *egg, beaten*
½ *teaspoon paprika*

Have butcher cut a pocket in the breast of veal, and also have him remove the bones if desired. This is not a meaty cut, and the bones are nice for nibbling, so boning is optional.

Sauté onions in chicken fat until golden. Stir in bread crumbs, diced apple, salt, pepper, and rosemary. Remove from heat and stir in beaten egg. Fill the cavity of the breast of veal with this mixture. Place roast in an open pan and sprinkle with paprika. Roast at 325 degrees until well done, basting occasionally with pan drippings. Takes about 30 minutes to the pound.
Serves 6.

SWEET AND SOUR TONGUE

1 *pickled beef tongue, about*
  4 pounds
1 *large onion, sliced*
1 *cup canned tomatoes*
Juice of 1 lemon
¼ *cup brown sugar*
2 *cups water*

½ *teaspoon salt*
3 *peppercorns*
4 *whole cloves*
1 *small clove garlic*
¼ *teaspoon cinnamon*
½ *cup raisins*

Pour about 1 quart boiling water over tongue in a deep saucepan, and boil for 10 minutes. Pour off water and remove tough skin. Put onion, tomatoes, lemon juice, and brown sugar into saucepan, stirring together. Add 2 cups of water. Return tongue to this pot and simmer for 1 hour. Add the salt, peppercorns, cloves, and garlic, and simmer until tender (about 3 hours) adding more water if necessary to keep meat covered. Remove the tongue from the sauce and let it cool; strain the sauce through a

food mill or through a coarse strainer. Return sauce to pot and add raisins, simmering a few minutes until raisins are tender. If a stronger sweet and sour taste is desired, add additional lemon juice and sugar until desired balance is achieved. Slice the cooled tongue and return to sauce. Serve hot slices covered with raisin sauce.
Serves 6–8.

BARBECUED LAMB RIBLETS

3 *pounds lamb riblets*
2 *tablespoons cooking oil*
1 *onion, sliced*
1 *clove garlic, minced*
1 *small can tomato sauce*
2 *tablespoons vinegar*
2 *tablespoons lemon juice*

2 *tablespoons brown sugar*
1 *tablespoon Worcestershire sauce*
1 *teaspoon dry mustard*
1 *teaspoon salt*
¼ *teaspoon Tabasco sauce*

Sauté onion and garlic in oil. Add tomato sauce, vinegar, lemon juice, brown sugar, Worcestershire sauce, mustard, salt, and Tabasco sauce. Stir and simmer for 15 minutes. Trim excess fat from riblets and arrange on broiler pan, brush with half the sauce, and broil until browned. Turn over, brush with remaining sauce, and broil until done.
Serves 6.

LAMB CHOPS A L'ORANGE

6 *large shoulder lamb chops, cut 1 inch thick*
¼ *cup matzo meal*
¼ *teaspoon salt*
⅛ *teaspoon pepper*
2 *tablespoons peanut oil*
¼ *teaspoon ginger*

1 *cup orange juice*
1 *tablespoon grated orange rind*
2 *tablespoons sugar*
2 *oranges, peeled and sectioned*

Coat lamb chops with matzo meal. Sprinkle with salt and pepper. Brown in hot peanut oil in a large skillet. Add mixture of ginger, orange juice, orange rind, and sugar. Cover and simmer for about 45 minutes, or until tender, basting occasionally. Add orange sections and heat a few minutes.
Serves 6.

LAMB STEW

½ *cup cooking oil*
2 *pounds cubed lamb*
3 *onions, sliced*
1 *clove garlic, crushed*
1 *teaspoon salt*

½ *teaspoon pepper*
2 *cups canned tomatoes*
½ *teaspoon oregano*
1 *teaspoon sugar*

Heat oil in a skillet. Brown cubes of meat on all sides. Add sliced onion and crushed garlic and simmer until onions are golden. Add remaining ingredients. Stir together. Simmer covered for 2 hours, adding water if sauce becomes too thick.
Serves 6.

ROAST SHOULDER OF LAMB

4-*pound rolled shoulder of*
  lamb roast
¼ *cup flour*
½ *teaspoon salt*
¼ *teaspoon pepper*
½ *teaspoon paprika*
2 *onions, sliced*
1 *clove garlic*

¼ *cup cooking oil*
3 *cups water*
¼ *cup vinegar*
¼ *cup catsup*
2 *tablespoons brown sugar*
1 *teaspoon Worcestershire*
  sauce

Combine flour, salt, pepper, and paprika; pat into surface of lamb roast. In a Dutch oven, brown onions and garlic in oil

and sear lamb roast on all sides. Combine the water, vinegar, catsup, brown sugar, and Worcestershire sauce. Pour over lamb roast. Cover tightly and roast in 350-degree oven for 2 hours, basting occasionally. Remove cover for last ½ hour to brown roast.
Serves 4–6.

STUFFED DERMA

6 *feet of beef casings,*
  cleaned
2 *cups flour*
⅔ *cup chicken fat*

2 *onions, grated*
1 *teaspoon salt*
½ *teaspoon pepper*
¼ *teaspoon celery salt*

Cut casings into 1-foot lengths. Tie 1 end of each casing, and turn inside-out. Combine flour, chicken fat, grated onions, salt, pepper, and celery salt. Stuff casings loosely with this mixture and tie open ends. Drop casings into boiling water for 5 minutes; remove, and scrape exteriors. Place in a greased roasting pan and bake in a 325-degree oven for 2 hours, or until well browned. Baste frequently with fat. Serve with meat or poultry in place of potato.
Makes 3 dozen 2-inch slices.

"A woman of valour who can find?
For her price is far above rubies."

BOOK OF PROVERBS

Have a Piece of Chicken

With so much talk about the Jewish mother and her chicken soup, one almost forgets to ask, what happens to the chicken? Since most of its strength and flavor has been absorbed into the soup, it is usually served as plain boiled chicken. Some cooks try to perk up the flavor by adding some paprika and roasting the chicken a bit before serving, but this dish is a tired offering when compared to the roasted chicken of Friday night fame.

Friday dinner traditionally calls for chicken as the main course, but many Jewish mothers will vary the menu occasionally and serve roast duckling or turkey. They may be filled with a potato-matzo stuffing or a fruit stuffing, two special favorites. Roast goose, while not as popular as it once was in the days of peasant cooking, is still relished in many homes. Chicken Fricassee, made with giblets, wings, and tiny meat balls, if often served as a *forshpeis* or as the main course on a mound of well-flavored rice.

Aside from having to use only poultry which has been slaughtered under ritual supervision, the Jewish cook is not hampered by other restrictions. She uses current recipes as long as they do not have *milchig* ingredients, and has even become adept in preparing Southern and Oriental inspired chicken dishes.

The recipes in this chapter adhere to the traditional methods of preparing poultry which are used by experienced *balabustas* throughout the world.

RENDERED CHICKEN FAT

Lumps of raw chicken fat   1 *onion, diced**
Water

Place fat in a heavy skillet. If *grebenes* are desired, add cut up pieces of fatty skin. (*Grebenes*, another word for cracklings, are crisp, browned bits of chicken skin, eaten with rye bread.) Cover fat with cold water, boil, then simmer covered for about 20 minutes. Uncover and cook over low heat until fat is melted and water is evaporated. Add diced onion, cooking until golden, just for flavor. Strain fat and refrigerate. Serve *grebenes* hot. Use rendered chicken fat in *fleishig* recipes in place of cooking fat to get traditional flavor.

* Use 1 small onion for each ½ pound raw fat.

ROAST CHICKEN

4- to 6-pound whole chicken,
   cleaned
2 tablespoons chicken fat

1 teaspoon paprika
½ teaspoon salt

Place cleaned chicken in a roasting pan. Combine fat, paprika, and salt. Rub chicken with this mixture. Roast at 325 degrees for about 2½ hours, or until tender.
Serves 8.

STEWED CHICKEN

2 whole frying chickens
1 can whole tomatoes
1 can tomato paste
1 can chicken broth, or
   2 cups chicken stock
2 sprigs fresh dill
½ teaspoon salt
¼ teaspoon pepper

1 pressed clove garlic
1 tablespoon sugar
2 onions, sliced
Paprika
1 cup sauterne wine
   (optional)
½ cup cold water
1 tablespoon cornstarch

Place whole chickens in a large Dutch oven. Add tomatoes, tomato paste, chicken broth, dill, salt, pepper, garlic, and sugar. Arrange slices of onion over all. Sprinkle with paprika. Add wine if desired. Cover and simmer for 1½ hours, or until tender. Remove chicken and thicken gravy by mixing cornstarch with cold water. Stir in ¼ cup hot gravy and return entire mixture to pot. Stir and simmer until gravy comes to a boil and is thickened. Serve with cut-up chicken.
Serves 6.

CHICKEN FRICASSEE

Wings, necks, backs, gizzards,
  and hearts of 2 chickens
¼ cup flour
2 onions, diced
¼ cup chicken fat
1 cup boiling chicken stock

½ pound lean ground beef
1 egg, beaten
¼ cup cold water
¼ teaspoon salt
⅛ teaspoon pepper
1 tablespoon chopped parsley

Dredge chicken parts in flour. Sauté onions in chicken fat in a deep saucepan. Add chicken parts and brown on all sides. Add chicken stock, cover, and simmer. Combine ground beef, beaten egg, water, salt, pepper, and chopped parsley. Form tiny meat balls and add to chicken. Cook for 20 minutes over a very low heat. To thicken gravy, combine 1 tablespoon of flour with ¼ cup cold water, add 2-3 tablespoons of hot gravy to this mixture and then pour into the pot while stirring and stir until a boiling point is reached and gravy thickens. Add salt and pepper to your taste. Serve on rice if desired. Serve as a main course.
Serves 4.

CHICKEN PAPRIKASH

2 fryers, cut into serving
  pieces
½ teaspoon salt
2 tablespoons chicken fat
  or oil

1 onion, sliced
1 tablespoon paprika
1 cup bouillon or chicken
  stock
1 teaspoon sugar

Salt the chicken pieces. In a Dutch oven, simmer sliced onion in chicken fat until transparent. Add paprika. Add chicken and lightly brown, turning constantly. Add bouillon and sugar. Cover and simmer for 1 hour, or until chicken parts are tender. If thicker gravy is desired, stir a teaspoon of flour into ½ cup water, add 2-3 tablespoons of hot gravy. Then pour into chicken liquid and simmer until thickened; stir constantly.
Serves 6.

ORANGE-GLAZED CHICKEN

4 *pounds cut-up chicken*
1 *teaspoon salt*
½ *teaspoon garlic salt*
1 *cup orange juice*
1 *cup light brown sugar*

1 *tablespoon* grated orange
rind
2 *tablespoons margarine*
1 *teaspoon dry mustard*
¼ *teaspoon ground allspice*
1 *orange, sliced*

Season chicken parts with salt and garlic salt and set aside. In a saucepan, combine the remaining ingredients and simmer for several minutes, stirring constantly. Place chicken parts in a roasting pan and cover with the glaze. Bake uncovered in a 350-degree oven, basting frequently until well-browned, about 1 hour. When half done, place a slice of fresh orange on each piece. *Serves* 4.

HONEY-BROILED CHICKEN

2 *broilers, split*
Juice of 2 lemons
½ *teaspoon salt*
¼ *teaspoon pepper*
½ *cup honey*

¼ *pound margarine*
1 *teaspoon dried tarragon*
1 *clove garlic, peeled and*
mashed

Sprinkle both sides of broilers with lemon juice, salt, and pepper. Brush both sides lightly with honey. Blend margarine, tarragon, and garlic together. Spread half of the mixture over the side of chicken facing broiler; broil 10 minutes. Turn and spread remaining mixture on other side of chicken. Broil an additional 10 minutes, or until done.
Serves 4.

ROCK CORNISH HENS WITH MATZO STUFFING

6 Rock Cornish hens
½ cup chicken fat
½ cup diced onion
1 cup diced mushrooms,
  fresh or canned
6 matzos, finely broken
¾ teaspoon salt

⅛ teaspoon pepper
1 tablespoon paprika
1 egg, slightly beaten
1 can condensed clear
  chicken soup
Chicken fat

Sauté onion and mushrooms in fat until tender but not browned. Add broken matzos and toast lightly. Combine salt, pepper, paprika, egg, and soup. Add to matzo mixture. Lightly fill body cavities with stuffing. Close openings with skewers. Brush liberally with chicken fat. Roast uncovered in a hot (425-degree) oven, brushing occasionally with additional fat, for 1 hour, or until tender.
Serves 6.

ROAST DUCKLING WITH POTATO-MATZO STUFFING

1 tablespoon soft chicken fat
½ teaspoon paprika
1 teaspoon salt
1 duckling, about 5 pounds
1½ pounds raw potatoes
1 onion
1 teaspoon salt

¼ teaspoon pepper
1 tablespoon dried parsley
  flakes, or 2 tablespoons fresh
2 eggs, beaten
½ cup matzo meal
¼ cup finely diced celery
½ teaspoon paprika

Combine chicken fat, paprika, and 1 teaspoon salt, and rub inside of duckling. Grate potatoes and onion and mix with 1 teaspoon salt, pepper, and parsley flakes. Add the beaten eggs. Add the matzo meal and diced celery. Stuff loosely into the cavity of the duckling. Sprinkle paprika over outer skin of duckling. Roast at 325 degrees for about 2½ hours, using a rack if possible.
Serves 4.

ROAST DUCKLING WITH ORANGE-PRUNE STUFFING

5-pound duckling, cleaned
2 teaspoons salt
½ teaspoon garlic powder
2 oranges
8 large prunes, pitted

1 egg
½ cup bread crumbs
1 tablespoon brown sugar
2 crushed gingersnaps

Combine salt and garlic powder; rub mixture over duckling on the outside and in the cavity. Chop the pulp of the oranges and the prunes. Add the egg, bread crumbs, brown sugar, and crushed gingersnaps. Stuff the mixture into the cavity loosely and close the opening with skewers or thread. Roast on a rack in a roasting pan at 425 degrees for 15 minutes, then at 350 degrees for about 2 hours, or until tender and browned. Baste skin with drippings occasionally.
Serves 4.

ROAST TURKEY

12- to 14-pound turkey, cleaned
¼ cup chicken fat
1 tablespoon paprika

1 teaspoon salt
½ teaspoon garlic salt

Combine chicken fat, paprika, salt, and garlic salt. Place turkey in a large roasting pan and rub all over with the seasoned fat. Rub salt in the cavity if you are not stuffing the bird. Roast in a 350-degree oven for 3½ hours, or until leg joint moves freely. Baste frequently with pan juices.
Serves 6–8.

· 10 ·

*"My fruit is better than gold, yea, than fine gold.
And my produce than choice silver."*

BOOK OF PROVERBS

Vegetables,
From Out of This World

A *tzimmes* is a casserole of mixed vegetables or fruits. In colloquial Yiddish it generally refers to a fuss over something, usually in a negative manner, such as, "Don't make a *tzimmes* out of it." However, there is nothing negative about a potato *tzimmes*; you will positively love it.

You will notice that in this chapter we carefully avoid plain steamed vegetables in hopes that you have already mastered the art of simple vegetable cookery or at least have learned to open cans and packages of vegetables with the best of us. We concentrate here on traditional vegetable concoctions, many of them meals in themselves.

What is Friday night dinner if a potato *tzimmes* or *kugel* doesn't accompany the chicken? Or Chanukah without crisp, hot potato *latkes* and cold applesauce? Learn to make these three dishes and you will be considered not only a *balabusta* but a *mavin*, a connoisseur of the best of Jewish cookery.

SWEET AND SOUR GREEN BEANS

2 *packages frozen French-cut green beans*
½ *teaspoon salt*
¼ *teaspoon pepper*
2 *onions, sliced paper thin*

1 *bay leaf*
1 *tablespoon sugar*
1 *tablespoon butter*
1 *tablespoon vinegar*

Place frozen beans in a saucepan. Cover bottom of pan with water. Add salt, pepper, sliced onions, and bay leaf, and simmer until beans are softened. Add sugar, butter, and vinegar, and simmer until beans are finished cooking. Remove bay leaf.
Serves 6.

GLAZED CARROTS

2 *pounds fresh carrots*
1 *cup boiling water*
1 *bouillon cube*

¼ *cup butter or margarine*
2 *tablespoons sugar*
1 *tablespoon chopped parsley*

Wash, scrape, and slice carrots into thick chunks. Dissolve bouillon cube in boiling water. Add carrots, butter, and sugar. Stir and simmer for 30 minutes until liquid is almost evaporated. Sprinkle with chopped parsley.
Serves 4–6.

CARROT PUDDING

3 cups grated raw carrots
¾ cup matzo meal
2 eggs, slightly beaten
¼ cup minced onion
1 teaspoon salt

2 tablespoons rendered chicken
fat or pareve margarine
1 can condensed clear chicken
soup, undiluted
2 teaspoons minced parsley

Combine carrots and matzo meal with beaten eggs. Add onion, salt, and fat. Stir in condensed chicken soup and parsley. Mix well. Pour into greased 1½-quart baking dish and bake in 325-degree oven for 50 minutes, or until firm.
Serves 6.

SAUERKRAUT

1 large head cabbage
2 teaspoons salt

Boiling water
2 1-quart canning jars

Remove tough outer leaves of cabbage. Cut into quarters and shred very fine. Pack the cabbage very tightly into the quart jars; add a teaspoon of salt to each and fill to the top with boiling water. Seal immediately and store for 3 weeks in a cool dry place, checking occasionally to be sure the caps stay tightly closed. After about 3 weeks, the sauerkraut should be properly fermented.
Makes 2 quarts.

SWEET AND SOUR RED CABBAGE

1 medium head red cabbage,
shredded
2 cups water
2 tablespoons brown sugar
Juice of 1 lemon

1 tablespoon vinegar
4 whole cloves
½ teaspoon ginger
½ teaspoon salt

Put shredded cabbage in a deep saucepan. Add water. Add sugar, lemon juice, vinegar, cloves, ginger, and salt. Cover and simmer until cabbage is tender.
Serves 6.

A fine cook and talented hostess, my friend Mona generously opened her private recipe collection to me. Her recipe for potato-stuffed cabbage was one of several selected for this book. It is, I think, a most delicious contribution.

POTATO-STUFFED CABBAGE

1 *large head cabbage*	2 *eggs, beaten*
5 *pounds potatoes, peeled*	½ *cup chicken fat*
2 *onions*	1 *#2½ can tomatoes*
½ *cup raw rice*	1 *teaspoon salt*
1 *teaspoon salt*	1 *tablespoon sugar*
½ *teaspoon pepper*	

Parboil cabbage and separate leaves. Trim heavy center line of each leaf. Set aside several large outer leaves. Grate potatoes and the small cabbage leaves near the core. Grate one of the onions. Combine the potatoes, grated cabbage, grated onion, raw rice, 1 teaspoon salt, pepper, and beaten eggs. Add melted chicken fat. Fill each cabbage leaf with about 2 tablespoons of the filling. Fold the bottom over filling, fold sides in, and roll up.

Line the bottom of a Dutch oven with the large outer cabbage leaves. Slice an onion into the pot. Add the tomatoes, 1 teaspoon salt, and sugar. Place rolled stuffed cabbage leaves into the pot. Add water if sauce becomes too thick. Cook over low heat for about 5 hours.
Serves 8.

MILCHIG STUFFED CABBAGE

1 *large leafy head cabbage*
3 *cups cooked rice*
2 *eggs, beaten*
1 *cup white raisins*
1 *tablespoon sugar*
1 *teaspoon cinnamon*
½ *teaspoon salt*
1 *#2½ can tomatoes*

1 *cup brown sugar*
2 *tablespoons vinegar*
Juice of 1 lemon
1 *onion, sliced*
1 *apple, sliced thin*
½ *teaspoon salt*
5 *crumbled gingersnaps*

Parboil cabbage. Cut around the core, and carefully remove leaves one by one. Trim heavy center lines. Combine cooked rice, beaten eggs, raisins, sugar, cinnamon, and salt. Place about 2 tablespoons of rice mixture in center bottom of each cabbage leaf; fold over, fold in each side, and roll up. Cut up extra cabbage leaves and place in bottom of a deep pot. Add can of tomatoes, brown sugar, vinegar, lemon juice, onion and apple slices, gingersnaps, and salt. Place rolled cabbage leaves open side down into the pot. Simmer covered for 2 hours.
Serves 6–8.

BAKED CAULIFLOWER

1 *large head cauliflower*
3 *eggs, beaten*
½ *cup chopped onion*
½ *cup chopped fresh parsley*
1 *clove garlic, minced*
1 *cup canned tomatoes*

½ *cup salad oil*
1 *teaspoon salt*
¼ *teaspoon pepper*
¾ *cup grated Parmesan*
   cheese

Discard leaves and hard core of cauliflower. Break into small flowerets and wash thoroughly. Blend all ingredients together, reserving ¼ cup grated Parmesan cheese for topping. Pour the mixture into a greased 1-quart casserole or flat baking dish, and sprinkle the reserved cheese over the top. Bake for 30 minutes at 400 degrees.

Serves 4–6.

PICKLED CUCUMBERS

2 *large cucumbers*
1 *large onion, sliced paper thin*
1 *cup vinegar*
½ *cup water*

2 *tablespoons salad oil*
2 *teaspoons sugar*
1 *teaspoon salt*
½ *teaspoon pepper*

Peel cucumbers and run the tines of a fork lengthwise down each to give it serrated edges when sliced. Slice paper thin. Place in a small deep bowl alternating with layers of onions. Combine vinegar, water, salad oil, sugar, salt, and pepper. Pour over cucumbers and refrigerate covered for several hours or overnight. Serve as a side dish.

Serves 6.

FRIED EGGPLANT

1 *eggplant, 1½ to 2 pounds*
1 *teaspoon salt*
2 *cups cold water*

2 *cups cornmeal*
1 *cup peanut oil*

Peel eggplant. Slice lengthwise about ½ inch thick and place in a deep bowl. Combine salt and water and pour over slices. To keep the slices submerged weight them down with a smaller bowl. Soak for ½ hour. Remove from water and pat dry with paper towels. Dip into cornmeal and fry in heated peanut oil in a large skillet. After frying, place slices on sheets of paper toweling to drain off excess oil.

Serves 4.

EGGPLANT-COTTAGE CHEESE CASSEROLE

3 tablespoons peanut oil or
   melted butter
1 large onion, sliced thin
1 medium eggplant (1½
   pounds)
¼ cup diced green pepper
1 can tomato and mushroom
   sauce

1 teaspoon salt
¼ teaspoon pepper
2 large tomatoes, peeled and
   cubed
1 pound cottage cheese
1½ cups matzo farfel, or
   2 crumbled matzos

Sauté onion in fat until tender. Pare eggplant and cut into ½-inch
cubes. Combine onion, eggplant, green pepper, tomato and mushroom sauce, salt, and pepper. Cover and cook 15 minutes, or
until eggplant is tender. Stir in tomatoes. In a greased 2-quart
baking dish, arrange alternate layers of the vegetables, cheese,
and matzo *farfel*, beginning and ending with the vegetables.
Bake uncovered in a 350-degree oven for 20 minutes.
Serves 6.

POTATO SALAD

3 pounds potatoes
3 hard-cooked eggs
1 cup celery, diced thin
2 onions, sliced paper thin
1 teaspoon salt

½ cup mayonnaise
½ cup sour cream
1 tablespoon vinegar
1 teaspoon sugar

Boil potatoes until soft but firm. Peel and cut into small wedges.
Shell eggs and slice into potatoes. Add celery, onions, and salt.
Mix well. Combine mayonnaise, sour cream, vinegar, and sugar.
Pour over potato mixture and stir to coat thoroughly. Refrigerate
until serving time.
Serves 6–8.

POTATO-CARROT KUGEL

2 cups grated raw potatoes
½ cup grated raw onion
¾ cup grated raw carrots
½ teaspoon salt
¼ teaspoon pepper

½ cup flour
3 tablespoons salad oil
2 eggs, beaten
1 tablespoon grated lemon
   rind

Combine grated potatoes, onions, and carrots. Add salt, pepper, and flour. Stir in salad oil. Stir in beaten eggs. Add grated lemon rind. Bake in greased flat baking pan at 375 degrees for 35 to 45 minutes, or until lightly browned. Cut in squares.
Serves 6.

LATKES (POTATO PANCAKES)

2 pounds potatoes, pared
2 onions
1 egg, slightly beaten
2 tablespoons flour

½ teaspoon salt
¼ teaspoon pepper
1 cup peanut oil

Grate potatoes into a deep bowl. Grate onions and add to potatoes. Add the egg, flour, salt, and pepper. Heat oil in a large skillet. Drop large spoonfuls of mixture into the hot oil and fry as pancakes. Serve with applesauce or sour cream.
Serves 6.

POTATO DUMPLINGS

3 large potatoes, peeled and
   grated
½ teaspoon salt

¼ teaspoon pepper
1 tablespoon melted fat
2 tablespoons flour

Strain or squeeze grated potatoes in cheesecloth to remove excess water. Add salt and pepper. Stir in melted fat and then stir in the flour. Form into balls the size of ping-pong balls. Drop carefully into gravy with potted meat to cook for about the last 2 hours of meat cooking time. Keep covered during cooking. *Makes 1 dozen.*

STEWED TOMATOES

6 *tomatoes, washed and quartered*
1 *onion, sliced thin*
½ *teaspoon salt*
¼ *teaspoon pepper*

1 *teaspoon sugar*
1 *teaspoon lemon juice*
2 *tablespoons fine bread crumbs*
½ *cup water*

Place tomatoes in a small, heavy saucepan. Add sliced onion, salt, pepper, sugar, and lemon juice. Add bread crumbs and water. Cover tightly, and simmer for 20 minutes, stirring occasionally and adding more water if necessary to keep from sticking. *Serves 4.*

PLAIN TZIMMES

2 *medium-size white potatoes*
2 *medium-size sweet potatoes*
2 *large carrots*

½ *cup chicken fat*
1 *cup chopped onions*
1 *teaspoon salt*

Wash and pare the potatoes and cook with the carrots until tender. Heat the fat in a skillet, add the onions, and sauté until tender brown. Mash the vegetables together with the browned onion and remaining fat in skillet, adding salt to taste. Turn into a baking dish and slip under the broiler until the top of the *tzimmes* is golden brown. *Serves 4.*

CARROT-FRUIT TZIMMES

1 1-*pound can whole baby carrots*
1 *small can pineapple tidbits*
1 1-*pound jar pitted prunes*
1 *tablespoon brown sugar*
Juice of ½ lemon

Combine drained juices of the carrots, pineapple, and prunes. Add sugar and lemon juice. Simmer for several minutes, to thicken slightly. Add whole carrots, pineapple tidbits, and pitted prunes. Simmer several minutes before serving as a hot side dish to a meat or chicken dinner.
Serves 4–6.

YAM TZIMMES

4 *tablespoons cooking oil*
4 *tablespoons chopped onion*
2 *pounds lean stew beef chunks*
1 *teaspoon salt*
¼ *teaspoon pepper*
1 1-*pound, 1-ounce jar pitted prunes*
4 *whole cloves*
1 *teaspoon cinnamon*
1 1-*pound, 7-ounce can yams, sliced lengthwise and drained*

Sauté the chopped onion in oil; add meat and brown. Season with salt and pepper. Cover and cook over low heat for about 15 minutes. Add pitted prunes with juice. Add cloves, cinnamon, and yams. Cover and simmer about 30 minutes, or until meat is tender.
Serves 6.

CARROT-YAM TZIMMES

4 1-*pound cans sliced carrots*
2 1-*pound cans sliced yams*
2 *tablespoons margarine*
1 *cup dried prunes and apricots*
1 *tablespoon lemon rind*
2 *tablespoons honey*

Into a greased casserole, empty the drained sliced carrots and yams. Dot with margarine. Top with prunes and apricots, lemon rind, and honey. Bake at 350 degrees for 30 minutes.
Serves 8.

WILD RICE RING

1 *cup raw wild rice*   1 *pound mushrooms*
1 *teaspoon salt*   ¼ *cup butter*
4 *cups water*

Wash raw rice thoroughly; boil in salted water about 45 minutes. Drain. Grind or chop mushrooms and sauté in butter for 5 minutes. Blend with the rice. Pour into a buttered 1-quart ring mold. Set in a pan of hot water and bake for 30 minutes at 350 degrees. Turn out on a platter and fill center with a cooked green vegetable. Garnish with cooked carrots and parsley around the rim.
Serves 4.

· 11 ·

"He that honoureth his mother,
Is as one that layeth up treasure."
JESHU BEN SIRAH

All Kinds of Noodles

How can anyone resist a tasty noodle pudding? Finer than pasta because of the addition of eggs to the dough, oozing with rich cheeses or fruits, noodle pudding is truly a *meichel*. What is a *meichel?* It is a delicious dish, concocted to charm the senses.

Where the only *milchig* ingredient in the recipe is butter, pareve margarine may be substituted and the pudding served with a *fleishig* meal. However, many of the puddings are constructed with cheese and sour cream, and these dishes are intended as a main course for a *milchig* meal.

A recipe for homemade noodles is given on page 35, and they may be used in place of the packaged noodles suggested in the following recipes. Simply cut the noodles wider than for soup accompaniments, dry them, and proceed with the instructions.

Once you have experienced the taste of these delicious puddings, you may be inspired to experiment, using other fruits and cheeses as substitutes for the ingredients listed. A true *balabusta* develops an instinct for exchanging ingredients on the theory of, "What could be bad?" Enjoy!

APPLE-NOODLE PUDDING

1 8-*ounce package wide
   noodles*
1 *tablespoon sugar*
1 *teaspoon cinnamon*

3 *eggs, separated*
1 *tablespoon butter*
3 *apples, peeled and sliced
   thin*

Boil and drain noodles as per directions on box. Add sugar and cinnamon. Add slightly beaten egg yolks. Break butter into bits and stir through. Stir in apple slices. Beat egg whites stiffly and fold in carefully but thoroughly. Bake in a greased casserole at 350 degrees for 1 hour.
Serves 4–6.

APPLESAUCE-NOODLE PUDDING

1 8-*ounce package wide
   noodles, cooked and drained*
½ *pound cottage cheese*
1 *cup sour cream*

1 *cup applesauce*
3 *eggs, well beaten*
1 *teaspoon salt*
¼ *cup butter*

Stir cottage cheese, sour cream, and applesauce together. Add the eggs and salt. Break butter into tiny pieces and add to mixture. Fold in cooked noodles. Pour into a greased 1-quart casserole and bake in a 350-degree oven for 1 hour. Raise the heat to 400 degrees for the last 15 minutes to brown the pudding. *Serves* 6.

NOODLE-BROCCOLI CASSEROLE

1 8-*ounce package wide noodles, cooked and drained*
2 10-*ounce packages frozen chopped broccoli, cooked*
½ *cup grated sharp cheddar cheese*
2 *tablespoons butter*

1 *tablespoon flour*
¾ *cup cream*
½ *teaspoon salt*
1 *teaspoon Worcestershire sauce*
¼ *cup water drained from cooked broccoli*

Combine cooked noodles and broccoli. Mix grated cheddar cheese through. In a small saucepan, melt butter, add flour, and stir until thickened. Add cream, stirring constantly while sauce is thickening. Add salt, Worcestershire sauce, and broccoli water, simmering and stirring until thick. Pour sauce over the noodle-broccoli mixture and blend through thoroughly. Bake in a greased 1½-quart casserole for 30 minutes at 350 degrees. *Serves* 6.

Cabbage Noodle Pletzel *is a dish of Hungarian origin. This recipe was obtained at the insistence of a friend from her mother, Freda.*

CABBAGE NOODLE PLETZEL

2 *pounds of raw cabbage, cubed*
5 *onions, diced*
½ *cup butter*

½ *teaspoon salt*
¼ *teaspoon pepper*
1 8-*ounce package wide noodles, cooked and drained*

Place cubed cabbage and diced onions in a large skillet. Add butter, salt, and pepper. Simmer gently, covered, for 2 hours until tender. Add small amounts of water only if necessary. Cabbage should be browned and tender. Then combine with the drained cooked noodles. Cover tightly and simmer together for 15 minutes.
Serves 4–6.

COTTAGE CHEESE-NOODLE PUDDING

1 8-*ounce package wide*
   noodles, boiled and drained
3 *eggs*
½ *pound cottage cheese*
½ *pint sour cream*
½ *teaspoon salt*
½ *cup sugar*

Juice of ½ *lemon*
½ *cup white raisins*
6 *tablespoons butter*
¼ *cup cornflake crumbs*
¼ *cup ground toasted*
   almonds

Beat eggs; add cheese, sour cream, salt, sugar, lemon juice, and raisins. Fold cooked noodles into this mixture. Put half of butter in an 8-inch-by-12-inch baking dish; heat in a 350-degree oven until melted. Pour noodles into the baking dish; top with cornflake crumbs and almonds, and dot remaining butter over top. Bake 1 hour at 350 degrees.
Serves 6.

NOODLE-CHIVE CASSEROLE

1 8-*ounce package wide*
   noodles, boiled and drained
1 *cup sour cream*
2 *tablespoons butter*

2 *tablespoons flour*
1 *cup milk*
2 *tablespoons chopped chives*
1 *teaspoon dry mustard*

Blend sour cream into cooked noodles. In a small saucepan, melt butter, stir in flour, then slowly stir in milk, making a cream sauce. Add chopped chives and mustard. Stir in the noodle mixture. Bake in a greased casserole at 350 degrees for 20 minutes. *Serves* 4.

OLD-FASHIONED EGG NOODLE PUDDING

1 *pound fine egg noodles,*
   boiled and drained
1 *dozen eggs*
1 *teaspoon salt*

¼ *teaspoon pepper*
⅛ *teaspoon garlic salt*
¼ *pound butter*
Paprika

Beat eggs well and fold into cooked noodles. Add salt, pepper, and garlic salt. Break up butter and mix through. Pour into a 1½-quart casserole. Sprinkle top with paprika. Bake at 400 degrees for 1 hour until brown.
Serves 6–8.

NOODLE AND RAISIN PUDDING

1 *8-ounce package wide*
   noodles, boiled and drained
¼ *pound butter*
8 *ounces cottage cheese*
½ *cup sugar*

½ *teaspoon cinnamon*
½ *cup seedless raisins*
Juice and grated rind of
   ½ *lemon*
1 *cup evaporated milk*

Topping:
¼ *cup cornflake crumbs*
1 *teaspoon sugar*

¼ *teaspoon cinnamon*

Combine butter, cottage cheese, and sugar. Add cinnamon, raisins, lemon juice and rind. Stir in evaporated milk. Mix thoroughly with cooked noodles. Pour into a greased 1-quart cas-

serole. Sprinkle topping on pudding. Bake for 1 hour at 350 degrees.
Serves 6.

NOODLE PUDDING SUPREME

1 8-*ounce package medium*
   noodles, boiled and drained
4 *eggs, separated*
½ *cup sugar*
1 8-*ounce package cream*
   cheese

1 *pint sour cream*
1½ *cups milk*
1 #2 *can crushed pineapple*
½ *stick butter*

Topping (optional):
¼ *cup cornflake crumbs*
1 *teaspoon sugar*

¼ *teaspoon cinnamon*

Combine egg yolks, sugar, cream cheese, sour cream, and milk. Fold boiled noodles into sauce. Stir in drained pineapple and stiffly beaten egg whites. Melt butter in a 1-quart baking dish; pour in mixture and bake at 300 degrees for 1 hour, then at 350 degrees for additional ½ hour. Top can be sprinkled with cornflake crumbs, sugar, and cinnamon before baking, if desired.
Serves 6.

PINEAPPLE KUGEL

1 *pound wide noodles,*
   boiled and drained
3 *eggs*
½ *cup sugar*

1 *teaspoon cinnamon*
8 *drained pineapple rings*
¼ *cup brown sugar*
2 *tablespoons butter*

Beat eggs slightly; add sugar and cinnamon. Mix egg batter through cooked noodles. Pour into a buttered, flat 8-inch-by-11-inch pan. Arrange pineapple rings across the top. Sprinkle with brown sugar and dot with butter. Bake 30 minutes in a 350-degree oven until set and lightly browned. Serve hot.
Serves 8.

FARFEL STUFFING

1 *cup* farfel
¼ *cup warm water*
1 *small onion, chopped*
Chicken fat

½ *teaspoon salt*
1 *egg, beaten*
½ *cup chopped mushrooms,*
  fresh or canned

Mix the *farfel* and warm water. Add salt. Sauté onion in small amount of fat. Add onion to *farfel*. Add the beaten egg. Mix in the chopped mushrooms. Stuff poultry or breast of veal before roasting. Or bake as a pudding in a greased 1-quart casserole for 30 minutes in a 350-degree oven.
Makes 2 cups stuffing.
Serves 4 as an accompaniment.

· 12 ·

"It is better to dwell in a desert land
Than with a contentious woman."

BOOK OF PROVERBS

What To Do with Eggs

Eggs are considered to be *pareve*, a neutral food which can accompany either *milchig* or *fleishig* foods. However, if the slightest blood spot is detected, the egg may not be used, since the stain signifies the beginning of animal life. If eggs are found in the hen, they may be used only as a *fleishig* food even though the shells may have formed.

An inexpensive source of high protein, eggs play a significant role in Jewish cookery. They are used as the base of omelets, matzo pancakes, and all kinds of blintzes. Very similar to a crepe a blintz is a very thin pancake which is filled with cheese or fruit, rolled up and fried, and served with cold sour cream. Blintzes make a wonderful main course in a dairy meal, and they are frequently served as the *pièce de résistance* with snack-time coffee. A cook who can produce feather-light blintzes will win renown for her skill, and will be known forevermore as a *beryah*, a jewel of a *balabusta*.

LOX OMELET

½ *onion, sliced*
2 *eggs*

2 *slices lox (smoked salmon),*
  diced
Salt and pepper

Sauté onions until golden. Beat eggs and add lox. Pour over onions. Push mixture from side to side as it solidifies, and cook only until all liquid is firm. Turn out on an individual plate, seasoning with salt and pepper to taste.
Serves 1.

SALAMI OMELET

4 *eggs*
½ *onion, grated*
½ *cup diced salami*
¼ *teaspoon salt*

⅛ *teaspoon pepper*
1 *tablespoon margarine or*
  cooking oil

Beat eggs until blended. Add grated onion and diced salami. Add salt and pepper. Heat oil in a skillet. Pour in egg mixture. Turn heat low, cover tightly, and cook for several minutes until eggs are firmly set. Fold omelet over and remove from skillet with a large spatula.
Serves 2.

NEPTUNE EGG SCRAMBLE

1 1-pound jar gefilte fish
¾ cup chopped onion
¼ cup butter
8 eggs, beaten

½ cup milk
1 tablespoon lemon juice
¾ teaspoon salt
⅛ teaspoon pepper

Drain and mash fish with a fork. Sauté onion in butter until tender but not brown. Mix eggs with milk, lemon juice, salt, pepper, and fish. Add to onion mixture and cook over low heat, stirring frequently until eggs are firm.
Serves 6.

FANKUCHEN

3 eggs, separated
½ cup milk
½ teaspoon salt

2 teaspoons sugar
½ cup matzo meal
½ cup cooking oil

Beat yolks and add milk. Add salt, sugar, and matzo meal. Beat egg whites stiff and fold into batter. Heat oil in a heavy skillet. Drop heaping tablespoonfuls of batter into hot oil and fry on both sides. Serve immediately.
Makes about 10 pancakes.

MAMALIGA

3 eggs, beaten
½ cup milk
1 cup cottage cheese
1 teaspoon salt
½ teaspoon pepper

1 cup matzo meal
½ cup cooking oil
1 onion, finely diced
1 can tomato sauce

Combine eggs, milk, and cottage cheese. Add salt, pepper, and matzo meal. Shape into large flat patties. Heat cooking oil in a heavy skillet and fry patties till lightly browned on both sides. Remove from pan and arrange in a baking pan. Fry onions in oil that remains in skillet. Add tomato sauce and stir. Pour sauce over pancakes and bake in a 350-degree oven for 15–20 minutes. *Serves 4.*

MATZO BREI

2 *matzos, broken into small*   ¼ *cup chicken fat*
  pieces   3 *eggs*
½ *cup chopped onions*   1 *teaspoon salt*

Place matzos in colander. Pour 1 quart of boiling water over the matzos and drain well. Sauté the onions in the fat until golden but not brown. Beat the eggs, adding the salt and then the matzos. Mix well and pour over the onions. Cook over medium heat until golden brown, stirring and turning frequently to brown on all sides.
Serves 2–3.

BLUEBERRY-COTTAGE CHEESE PANCAKES

3 *eggs*   ¼ *teaspoon salt*
1 *cup cottage cheese, sieved*   1 *teaspoon grated lemon rind*
2 *tablespoons light salad oil*   1 *cup whole fresh blueberries*
¼ *cup flour*

Beat eggs until lemon-colored. Blend in sieved cottage cheese. Blend in salad oil. Add flour, salt, and lemon rind. Fold in washed, drained blueberries. Spoon onto a greased griddle. Turn once when bottoms are lightly browned. Serve at once, with powdered sugar or sour cream.
Makes about 1 dozen.

WINE CHREMSELS

1 cup matzo meal
1 cup sweet wine
4 eggs, separated
1 tablespoon chopped almonds

1 teaspoon sugar
½ cup peanut oil
Powdered sugar

Stir matzo meal into wine. Add beaten egg yolks, chopped almonds, and sugar. Beat egg whites stiff and fold into batter. Heat peanut oil in a skillet. Drop tablespoonfuls of batter into hot oil and fry until lightly browned. Remove and drain on paper toweling. Sprinkle with powdered sugar and serve immediately. *Makes about 2 dozen.*

GEFILTE FISH PUFF

4 eggs, separated
½ teaspoon salt
⅛ teaspoon pepper
¼ cup liquid from jar of
 gefilte fish

4 regular-size servings from
 jar of gefilte fish, mashed
¼ cup matzo meal
1 teaspoon finely chopped
 parsley
2 tablespoons butter or fat

Beat the egg yolks, salt, and pepper. Add the fish liquid. Fold in the mashed gefilte fish, matzo meal, and chopped parsley. Beat egg whites until stiff but not dry. Carefully fold the egg yolk mixture into the beaten egg whites. Heat butter or fat in a 9-inch skillet. Add the egg mixture and cook for about 5 minutes until the bottom of the puff is golden brown. Place the puff on a pan in broiler under low heat for about 5 minutes to brown and cook the top. When the gefilte fish puff is done, turn out on a heated platter, cut into four wedge shapes, and serve. *Serves 4.*

The easiest way to learn how to cook like a Jewish mother is to be born to one. My Mama Ida made cooking seem to be as easy as breathing. She is responsible for many of the good ideas throughout this book, but special credit must be given to her for this superb recipe for Cheese Blintzes. They are almost as unique as the lady who devised them.

CHEESE BLINTZES

Batter:

½ cup flour

½ teaspoon salt

2 eggs, well beaten

⅔ cup milk

1 tablespoon melted shortening

Sift flour, add salt, and sift again. Combine eggs, milk, and melted shortening. Add flour slowly to egg batter and beat until smooth.

Filling:

½ pound farmer cheese

½ pound cream cheese

1 egg, well beaten

2 tablespoons sugar

2 tablespoons melted butter

¼ teaspoon cinnamon

Mash the farmer cheese and cream cheese together. Add beaten egg. Add sugar, melted butter, and cinnamon. Blend well.

Brush a 6-inch skillet lightly with melted butter, heat it, and pour in just enough batter to cover the bottom of the skillet. Cook until firm and turn out on a clean dish towel, browning only one side of the crepe. When all the batter is used up, fill each crepe with about 2 tablespoons of cheese filling, placing the filling on the center of the browned side of the crepe and folding over the 2 opposite sides; then roll up the remaining sides to enclose the filling in the crepe. Brown in butter just before serving. Serve with sour cream.

Makes 1 dozen.

BLUEBERRY BLINTZES

Batter: See page 98.

Filling:

1 *cup blueberries, washed*	⅛ *teaspoon cinnamon*
2 *tablespoons sugar*	⅛ *teaspoon nutmeg*
2 *teaspoons cornstarch*	

Pick stems off blueberries and remove undersized or spoiled fruit. Sprinkle sugar and cornstarch over the rest. Add cinnamon and nutmeg, and shake until berries are thoroughly coated. Fill blintzes and roll up with ends tucked in. Fry in butter, or bake in a 350-degree oven until browned.
Makes 1 dozen.

· 13 ·

Ess From the Cookie Jar

The cookie jar filled with home-baked goodies will reveal more about the heart of the home than the well-planned decor. For a cookie jar plainly says, "Welcome. There are treats in store for you."

Assembled here are heirloom recipes for traditional and unusual cookies which require the loving care of a home kitchen to prepare. These cookies are never found in boxes and rarely in bakeries, but the happy hands that reach for them will make the effort worthwhile.

The recipes are designed to produce three or four dozen cookies at a time, so that your output will not be a taste-teaser but a source of repeated fulfillment. First, obtain a jar large enough to hold one baking, preferably made of glass, so that your baking will not be a secret. Then, equip yourself with several large cookie sheets to enable you to bake several relays from each recipe. However, bake only one panful at a time to be sure to get perfect heat circulation for each batch of cookies.

With your cookie jar full of delicious bait, stand back and count the happy fishermen!

CARROT COOKIES

½ *pound carrots, scraped and grated*
1 *cup sweet butter, softened*
3 *eggs, slightly beaten*
1 *cup flour*

2 *teaspoons baking powder*
½ *teaspoon salt*
½ *cup ground walnuts*
Cinnamon
Sugar

Combine grated carrots with softened butter. Blend in eggs. Sift flour, baking powder, and salt together. Blend into batter. Add ground walnuts and knead into dough. Roll out dough to a large ¼-inch-thick square. Sprinkle with cinnamon and sugar. Cut strips 2 inches wide, then cut across every inch. Place dough pieces on a greased cookie sheet and bake at 350 degrees for about 15 minutes, or until lightly browned.
Makes about 2 dozen cookies.

This recipe for orange cookies was contributed by a friend, Nola, who went to great lengths to persuade a member of her family to write it down. It is a most appreciated philanthropy, for the recipe is too good to be limited to word-of-mouth inheritance.

ORANGE COOKIES

1 1-pound can vegetable
  shortening
1¼ cups sugar
4 eggs
½ cup orange juice
½ cup seltzer
  (carbonated water)

1 teaspoon vanilla
4 cups flour
1 tablespoon baking powder
Sugar
Cinnamon

Cream shortening and sugar and add eggs. Add orange juice and seltzer. Add vanilla. Add flour and baking powder, kneading all together. Divide dough into 4 parts; roll each part about ¼ inch thick and cut with cookie cutter or the rim of a floured glass. Bake on greased cookie sheets at 350 degrees about 15 minutes or until slightly browned. Remove from oven and sprinkle with sugar and cinnamon.
Makes 4 dozen.

Rarely does a recipe come from daughter to mother, but Nancy took my favorite oatmeal cookies and turned them into an even more wonderful mouthful. And so a heritage moves onwards.

OATMEAL COOKIES

1 cup sweet butter
1 cup sugar
2 eggs, beaten
2 cups oatmeal
2 cups flour
1 teaspoon baking powder

½ teaspoon baking soda
¼ teaspoon salt
1 teaspoon cinnamon
¼ cup milk
1 cup seedless raisins
1 cup chocolate bits

Cream butter and sugar. Add eggs. Combine the dry ingredients: oatmeal, flour, baking powder, baking soda, salt, and cinnamon. Add gradually to the batter. Stir in milk. Stir in raisins and chocolate bits. The dough should be fairly stiff. Drop on a greased tin by the tablespoonful, about an inch apart. (If you prefer small cookies, use a teaspoon.) Bake at 350 degrees for 15-20 minutes, or until browned.
Makes 3 dozen.

PEANUT BUTTER COOKIES

½ *cup shortening*
½ *cup light brown sugar*
½ *cup peanut butter*
1 *egg*

½ *teaspoon salt*
1¼ *cups flour*
1 *teaspoon baking powder*

Blend shortening, sugar, and peanut butter together. Add egg. Add salt, flour, and baking powder, forming a stiff dough. In the palms of hands, roll dough into balls the size of a walnut. Press with floured or sugared fork, criss-cross. Bake at 350 degrees for about 12 minutes.
Makes about 3 dozen cookies.

WALNUT COOKIES

3 *cups flour*
1 *teaspoon baking soda*
2 *teaspoons salt*
1 *cup shortening*

2 *cups sugar*
2 *eggs*
2 *teaspoons vanilla*
1 *cup chopped walnuts*

Sift flour, baking soda, and salt together. Cream shortening at high speed with electric mixer until fluffy. Add sugar gradually and beat until creamy and light. Add eggs one at a time. Add

vanilla. Gradually add flour mixture at low speed until absorbed. Add nuts. Turn dough out on a large piece of waxed paper and form into a firm roll about 2 inches in diameter. Wrap and refrigerate overnight. To bake, slice into ¼-inch slices and bake on a greased cookie sheet, about 1 inch apart, at 375 degrees for 10 - 15 minutes, or until brown.
Makes about 4 dozen.

HAMANTASCHEN

Dough:

2 cups flour
1 teaspoon baking powder
⅓ cup sugar
⅛ teaspoon salt

Grated rind of 1 lemon
2 eggs
2 tablespoons cooking oil

Sift together flour, baking powder, sugar and salt. Add grated lemon rind. Break eggs into the center of the dry ingredients. Add oil, and mix all together, kneading lightly until smooth. Roll out on floured board; cut circles with cookie cutter or floured rim of a glass. Place a teaspoon of filling in each center and fold 3 sides of circle toward the middle, pinching edges together to form a tricornered shape. Bake on greased cookie sheets at 375 degrees for about 30 minutes, or until browned.
Makes 2 dozen.

Prune Filling:

½ pound pitted prunes
2 tablespoons grated orange
  rind

¼ cup chopped walnuts
2 tablespoons sugar
Dash of nutmeg

Cook prunes in small amount of water. Strain. Combine with rest of ingredients and chop fine. Fill dough and proceed as above.

Poppy Seed Filling:

⅛ pound poppy seeds
1 cup water
¼ cup sugar
¼ cup raisins

1 tablespoon honey
Dash of cinnamon
1 tablespoon grated orange
    rind

Put poppy seeds in water and simmer, covered, for 1 hour. Drain and grind or pound into a paste. Mix with the sugar, raisins, honey, cinnamon, and orange rind. Fill dough and proceed as above.

BROWNIES

4 eggs
2 cups sugar
⅞ cup sweet butter
4 squares unsweetened baking
    chocolate

1½ cups flour
1 teaspoon baking powder
1 teaspoon vanilla
1 cup chopped walnuts

Beat eggs. Add sugar and beat well. Melt butter and chocolate together and add to batter. Sift flour and baking powder together and add to batter. Add vanilla and walnuts. Spread batter in a greased square cake pan. Bake at 350 degrees for 25 minutes. Cool, and then cut into squares.
Makes about 2 dozen.

CINNAMON ROLLS

½ pound sweet butter
2 cups sugar
2 eggs
3 tablespoons sour cream
4 cups flour
1 cup crushed almonds

Grated rind of 1 lemon
½ teaspoon cinnamon
Sugar
Cinnamon
Fat for frying

Cream butter and sugar and add eggs. Add sour cream. Add flour. Then add almonds, grated lemon rind, and cinnamon. Knead dough and roll out ¼ inch thick. Cut into strips 1 inch wide and 4 inches long; roll up jelly-roll fashion. Fry in deep fat, lift out with a slotted spoon, and dip in a mixture of sugar and cinnamon.

Makes about 4 dozen.

PECAN ROLLS

3 *cups flour*
2 *tablespoons baking powder*
1 *teaspoon salt*

1 *cup sweet butter, softened*
¼ *cup sour cream*

Sift flour, baking powder, and salt together. Cut in slightly softened butter until consistency is mealy. Then add sour cream and work into a soft dough.

Roll out dough on a lightly floured pastry board, forming a rectangle ¼ inch thick. Spread filling over dough and roll up in jelly-roll fashion. Cut in ½-inch slices and place each slice cut-side up in a section of a buttered muffin tin. Bake at 375 degrees until glazed and golden brown, about 25 minutes.

Filling:
½ *cup brown sugar*
½ *cup butter*
½ *cup chopped pecans*

½ *cup seedless raisins*
1 *teaspoon cinnamon*

Cream brown sugar and butter thoroughly. Mix in pecans, raisins, and cinnamon.

Makes about 2 dozen rolls.

HONEY PECAN BARS

½ cup shortening
1 cup honey
6 egg yolks
1¼ cups flour, sifted
1 teaspoon baking powder

½ teaspoon salt
1 cup chopped dates
1 cup chopped pecans
1 teaspoon vanilla

Cream shortening and honey together. Add egg yolks, one at a time, beating well. Sift flour, baking powder, and salt together. Blend flour mixture into batter. Add chopped dates and pecans. Add vanilla. Spread into a greased, flat 9-inch-by-13-inch pan. Bake at 350 degrees for 30 minutes. Cool and cut into bars. *Makes about 3 dozen.*

When I think of a typical Jewish mother, I think of Aunt Rose, who not only holds her own family together but her brothers' and her sisters' children as well. A balabusta, summa cum laude, she generously donated this rugelach recipe as well as several others to this book.

CHEESE RUGELACH

½ pound cream cheese
½ pound sweet butter
½ pound cottage cheese,
   strained

1 teaspoon vanilla
1 tablespoon sugar
3 cups flour

Filling:
½ cup chopped nuts
1 cup seedless raisins

1 teaspoon cinnamon
½ cup sugar

Combine cream cheese, butter, and strained cottage cheese; blend well. Add vanilla and sugar. Work in flour. Roll dough into 4 circles, one at a time. Mix filling ingredients together and sprinkle evenly on each circle. Divide each circle into 8 parts, and roll from wide end to the point. Curve the roll gently into a "C" shape, forming a crescent with open end down. Bake at 350 degrees on a greased cookie sheet for 25 minutes, or until lightly browned.

Makes 32.

This sour cream rugelach *recipe has been streamlined for the modern kitchen, but it originated over a hundred years ago. It was told to me in confidence by a great philosopher and grass-roots psychologist, Tante Rifke, who would have shared her recipe with you too, if you were fortunate enough to know her.*

RUGELACH

5 *cups flour*
¾ *cup sugar*
3 *teaspoons baking powder*
1 *teaspoon salt*
1 *pound sweet butter*
2 *eggs*

1 *cup sour cream*
1 *1-pound jar apricot preserves*
½ *cup ground almonds*
¼ *cup sugar*
1 *tablespoon cinnamon*

Combine flour, sugar, baking powder, and salt. Cut in butter until mixture is mealy. Make a well in the center and add the eggs and sour cream; then knead into a dough. Refrigerate dough for at least 1 hour. Roll into 9-inch circles, using about ⅛ of the dough for each circle. Spread with apricot preserves and cut into 8 wedge-shaped sections, using a pizza cutter if you have one. Roll each wedge, starting from the large end and ending with the point; curve to form crescent-shaped rolls. Combine ground almonds, sugar, and cinnamon and dip each crescent into the mixture before placing on a greased cookie sheet. Bake at 375 degrees for about 15 minutes, or until browned.

Makes about 5½ dozen.

FRUIT AND NUT RUGELACH

1 *pound sweet butter*　　　3 *tablespoons sour cream*
½ *pound cream cheese*　　¼ *cup sugar*
3½ *cups flour*　　　　　　½ *teaspoon salt*

Cream butter and cream cheese together. Add flour. Add sour cream, sugar, and salt. Knead into a dough and refrigerate for several hours until firm. Roll into 9-inch circles, using about ⅙ of the dough for each circle. Spread with filling and cut into 8 wedge-shaped sections, using a pizza cutter if you have one. Roll each wedge, starting from the large end and ending with the point; curve to form crescent-shaped rolls with open end down. Bake at 375 degrees for about 15 minutes, or until browned.

Filling:
1 *1-pound jar orange marmalade*　½ *cup chopped walnuts*
½ *cup chopped seedless*
　raisins

Combine ingredients and spread on circles of dough before cutting and rolling.
Makes 4 dozen.

CHOCOLATE CONFECTION

2 *squares unsweetened*　　¾ *cup matzo meal*
　chocolate　　　　　　　1 *cup chopped walnuts*
1 *14-ounce can sweetened*
　condensed milk

Melt chocolate in the top of a double boiler over boiling water. Add condensed milk and stir until thickened, about 2 minutes. Remove from heat. Add matzo meal and chopped nuts. Mix well and press mixture into a buttered pan. Chill several hours in refrigerator. Cut into small squares.
Makes 2 dozen.

TEIGLACH No. 1

6 eggs
3 cups flour
1 teaspoon cinnamon
1 teaspoon ginger
¼ teaspoon salt

¼ cup chopped nuts
1½ cups honey
1 cup sugar
1 teaspoon ginger (optional)

Beat eggs. Blend flour, cinnamon, ginger, salt, and nuts together; add to beaten eggs, making a soft dough. With floured hands, roll dough into about 6 long ropes, about ½ inch in diameter. Cut each rope every ½ inch to get marble-sized pieces of dough. In a deep saucepan, heat the honey and sugar together; add another teaspoon of ginger to the mixture if desired. When the syrup is boiling, drop the pieces of dough in, one by one, to coat. Shake the pan gently to prevent the pieces from sticking together or sticking to the pan. Cover pot, reduce heat but keep it boiling, and cook until the dough is browned and puffed. Remove from heat and add 1 cup of boiling water to the pot, being careful not to spatter yourself. Remove the *teiglach* from the pot and pile onto a platter, or store in a covered crock with remaining syrup. *Makes about 3 dozen.*

TEIGLACH No. 2

2 eggs
½ cup oil
¼ cup water
2 teaspoons baking powder
3 cups flour

2 tablespoons grated lemon
rind
1½ cups honey
1 teaspoon ginger
¼ cup slivered almonds

Beat eggs, add oil and water. Add baking powder and flour and grated lemon rind, kneading together to make a dough. With floured hands, roll dough into long ropes, about ½ inch in diameter. Cut each rope every ½ inch and spread these pieces in a single layer in a well-floured roasting pan. Bake at 350 degrees until pieces are lightly browned, approximately 15 minutes.

In a deep saucepan, heat the honey and ginger. Drop in browned *teiglach* and cook until they are thoroughly coated. Add slivered almonds and mix through. Wet a pastry board, put the entire mixture on it and, with wet hands, flatten into a rectangular shape. Drop additional nuts over the surface, if desired, and let stand until dry. When dry enough to cut, cut into diagonal strips 1 inch by 2 inches.
Makes 3 dozen.

While applying layers of polish, my Hungarian manicurist told me about her mouth-watering yeast doughnuts and I invited her to contribute the recipe to this collection. These irresistible doughnuts are easy to make. They may be filled with whatever flavor jelly you prefer. Good to the last bite!

YEAST DOUGHNUTS

1¼ *cups milk*
2 *tablespoons sweet butter or*
  margarine
1 *package dry yeast*
¼ *cup lukewarm water*
2 *egg yolks*

4 *cups flour*
¼ *cup sugar*
Prune or apricot jelly
1 *quart oil*
Powdered sugar

Scald the milk and butter together; let cool. Dissolve the dry yeast in the lukewarm water. Add to cooled milk mixture. Beat egg yolks and add to batter. Stir flour and sugar together; slowly stir in liquid mixture until a dough has formed. Knead for 5 minutes. Let rise in a greased bowl for 1 hour. Punch down and divide dough in half. On a well-floured board, roll half the dough till ¼ inch thick. Cut rounds of dough with a glass; spoon 1 tablespoon jelly on each of half the rounds, using the other half to top the jelly. Press edges together. Roll out second half of dough and repeat procedure above. Fry doughnuts in deep hot oil until browned. Remove with a slotted spoon, drain on paper toweling to remove excess oil, and sprinkle with powdered sugar if desired.
Makes about 2 dozen.

·14·

A *Balabusta*'s Bake-Off

No bakery can include the ingredient of affection that a Jewish mother adds to her batter. Although her efforts will be quickly devoured, the crumbs of loving memory will remain. How can a bakery compete with the aroma of Friday's baking? And, if a lucky child gets to lick the batter bowl afterwards, he will never appreciate store-bought cake again.

The following collection of cakes, tortes, strudels, pies, and bread will create nostalgia forevermore. All of the recipes have been selected for their outstanding *tam*, and yet most are easy to prepare.

Several Passover recipes where matzo meal or potato flour is substituted for regular flour have also been included. While they may be used all year round, they are especially appreciated at Passover time when cakes with leavening may not be eaten.

The secret of successful baking is to have good quantities of ingredients on hand, an electric mixer, sturdy pans, and an ungrudging love of family. With all of this, these recipes are yours for the baking.

BLITZ KUCHEN

6 *egg yolks*	6 *egg whites, stiffly beaten*
¾ *cup sugar*	1 *12-ounce jar apricot*
⅔ *cup flour*	*marmalade*
1 *teaspoon lemon juice*	*Ground almonds (optional)*

Combine egg yolks and sugar and beat. Add flour gradually. Add lemon juice. Add 4 egg whites, reserving 2 egg whites for topping. Spread in 7½-inch-by-11-inch baking pan, shaping dough up the sides. Bake at 350 degrees for 20 minutes. Then remove from the oven and spread with apricot marmalade. Spread remaining beaten egg whites over marmalade and sprinkle with ground almonds if desired. Return to oven and bake for an additional 5 minutes, or until meringue is nicely browned.
Serves 8.

GUGELHUPF

½ *pound sweet butter,*	¾ *cup lukewarm milk*
softened	1 *teaspoon lemon juice*
2 *cups sugar*	1 *teaspoon grated lemon rind*
4 *eggs, separated*	1 *teaspoon vanilla*
3 *cups flour*	*Powdered sugar*
2 *tablespoons baking powder*	

Beat butter and sugar. Add egg yolks. Sift flour and baking powder 3 times. Add flour mix and milk alternately to batter. Add vanilla, lemon juice, and rind. Beat egg whites stiffly; fold carefully into batter. Grease an angel food pan. Fill with batter and bake for 5 minutes at 500 degrees, 5 minutes at 425 degrees, and 50 minutes at 325 degrees. Remove from oven and sprinkle with powdered sugar.
Makes 12 slices.

POPPY SEED CAKE

Prepare filling before making dough:

Filling:

¾ *pound ground poppy seeds*
Boiling water
1 *cup seedless raisins*
1 *tablespoon sugar*
¼ *cup dry cocoa*
1 *4-ounce package chocolate snap cookies (about 20)*

Mix enough boiling water, about 1 cup, into the ground poppy seeds to make a thick paste. Add raisins, sugar, cocoa, and crushed chocolate snap cookies. Add enough boiling water to make the mixture thick but spreadable.

Dough:

1½ *pounds sweet butter, softened*
½ *cup sugar*
2 *egg yolks*
6 *tablespoons evaporated milk*
4 *cups sifted flour*
1 *tablespoon baking powder*
1 *tablespoon melted butter*
1 *egg*
1 *tablespoon water*

Combine butter and sugar. Add egg yolks. Add evaporated milk. Sift flour and baking powder together. Add to dough, slowly working it in. Knead dough well. Divide in half and roll out about ½ inch thick. Spread melted butter over dough with a

brush; spread half the topping over dough and roll up jelly-roll fashion. Repeat with second half of dough. Beat an egg and add water, making an egg wash; brush tops of both loaves with wash. Bake in a small roasting pan or on cookie sheet in a 400-degree oven for 45 minutes.
Makes 2 loaves.

NUTCAKE

2 *cups sugar*
12 *egg yolks*
2 *cups grated almonds*
Juice of 1 *lemon*
Grated rind of 1 *lemon*

12 *egg whites, stiffly beaten*
1 *tablespoon flour*
½ *teaspoon baking powder*
2 *tablespoons ground nuts or fine bread crumbs*

Beat sugar and egg yolks together until lemon-colored. Add grated almonds. Add lemon juice and rind. To stiffly beaten egg whites, add flour and baking powder; then fold into yolk batter. Butter a 10-inch spring-form pan and dust lightly with ground nuts or fine bread crumbs. Fill with batter and bake for 45 minutes at 375 degrees.
Serves 8–10.

MANDEL TORTE

2 *cups ground almonds*
2 *cups sugar*
12 *egg yolks, beaten*

Grated peel of 1 *lemon*
12 *egg whites, stiffly beaten*

Butter a 10-inch spring-form pan and dust lightly with ½ cup ground almonds. Beat sugar and egg yolks until smooth. Add remaining ground almonds and grated lemon peel. Beat egg whites stiffly and fold into batter. Pour immediately into prepared pan and place in 400-degree oven for 30 minutes, or until firm. *Serves 8–10.*

The following recipes for butter doughs and their fillings were translated from a handwritten German notebook that a mother gave to her engaged daughter about one hundred years ago. The lady, who was the great-grandmother of my dear friend, Lenore, must have been a genius in the kitchen for she used her butter dough with great ingenuity. The yellowed pages were adapted to the American kitchen by another friend, Gerda, with infinite patience and skill. And so another mother-to-daughter confidence will live on for future generations of Jewish mothers, due to the generosity of people who are proud to perpetuate their heritage.

BASIC BUTTER DOUGH No. 1

3 cups flour   1 pound sweet butter
Pinch of salt   2 eggs, beaten

Combine the flour and salt with ½ pound butter, cutting together with a pastry cutter. Add beaten eggs and work dough until it has bubbles. Roll out dough and spread ¼ pound softened butter over half the dough. Fold the other half over, and top with the remaining ¼ pound butter. Fold dough over and roll flat, repeating rolling and folding process 3 times in all. Use dough as base for following recipes.

BASIC BUTTER DOUGH No. 2

3 cups flour   1 pound sweet butter,
Pinch of salt   softened
½ cup sour cream

Combine flour and salt. Using a pastry cutter, work sour cream and butter through, then knead to form a smooth dough. Roll out twice, each time folding dough into quarters and rolling again. Use dough as base for following recipes.

APPLE CAKE

Basic butter dough (see p. 116)
4 egg yolks
½ cup sweet cream
1 tablespoon sugar
1 teaspoon cinnamon
8 apples, peeled and sliced
½ cup slivered almonds
Powdered sugar

Spread butter dough in a 10-inch-by-14-inch pan, shaping dough part way up the sides. Combine egg yolks, sweet cream, sugar, and cinnamon. Spread mixture on top of butter dough. Arrange apples in rows on top. Sprinkle with slivered almonds. Bake in a 350-degree oven for 40 minutes, or until browned. Sprinkle with powdered sugar while cake is still hot.
Serves 12.

CHERRY CAKE

Basic butter dough (see p. 116)
4 cups sweet pitted cherries,
   or 2 cans cherry pie filling
4 eggs
½ cup sweet or sour cream
1 tablespoon sugar
1 teaspoon vanilla
½ teaspoon cinnamon
¼ cup slivered almonds

Topping (optional):
½ cup ground almonds
¼ cup sugar
1 teaspoon cinnamon

Roll dough thick and pat into a 10-inch-by-14-inch pan. Arrange cherries evenly over dough. Beat eggs, add cream, sugar, vanilla,

cinnamon, and slivered almonds. Pour over cherries. Bake in a
350-degree oven for 35 minutes. If desired, make topping by
combining almonds, sugar, and cinnamon, and sprinkle over top
of hot cake when it is removed from the oven.
Serves 12.

SWEET AND SOUR CHERRY CAKE

Basic butter dough (see p. 116)   ¾ *cup ground almonds*
2 *cups sour cherries, pitted*   ¼ *cup sugar*
2 *cups sweet cherries, pitted*   1 *teaspoon cinnamon*

Roll basic butter dough thick and pat into a 10-inch-by-14-inch
pan. Arrange sweet and sour cherries alternately over dough.
Shake ¼ cup ground almonds between the cherries. Combine the
remaining ½ cup ground almonds with the sugar and cinnamon
and sprinkle evenly over all. Bake for 35 minutes in a 350-degree
oven.
Serves 12.

CHERRY CAKE WITH TOPPING

Basic butter dough (see p. 116)   ½ *cup sugar*
4 *cups sweet cherries*   ½ *cup chopped almonds*
6 *eggs, separated*   *Grated peel of* 1 *lemon*

Roll basic butter dough thick and pat into a 10-inch-by-14-inch
pan. Arrange cherries over dough. Bake for 30 minutes at 350
degrees. Meanwhile, prepare topping by beating 6 egg yolks until
lemon-colored. Add sugar, beating until smooth. Add chopped
almonds and grated lemon peel. Beat egg whites stiff and fold
into the egg yolk batter. Remove cake from the oven, spread
topping quickly, return to the oven to brown, about 15 minutes
more.
Serves 12.

CREAM CAKE

Basic butter dough (see p. 116)
8 egg yolks
6 whole eggs
¼ pound sweet butter
Grated peel of 1 lemon

1 cup sweet cream
½ cup candied fruit
  (optional)
½ teaspoon cinnamon
¼ cup crushed almonds

Roll butter dough ¼ inch thick and pat into a 10-inch-by-14-inch pan. Beat egg yolks and whole eggs together until lemon-colored. Add softened butter and beat until smooth. Add lemon peel and sweet cream. Add candied fruit, cinnamon, and crushed almonds. Pour over butter dough. Bake for 30 minutes at 350 degrees. Serves 12.

ONION CAKE

Basic butter dough (see p. 116)
12 onions, sliced
3 tablespoons butter
½ teaspoon salt

6 eggs
½ cup sour cream
2 tablespoons caraway seed

Roll butter dough ½ inch thick. Pat into a 10-inch-by-14-inch pan. Sauté the sliced onions in butter until slightly golden and cool. Beat eggs and add sour cream. Add sautéed onions. Add salt and caraway seed. Pour onto dough. Bake at 350 degrees for 25 minutes, or until firmly set. Cut in squares to serve. Serves 12.

PLUM CAKE

Basic butter dough (see p. 116)
2 pounds fresh blue freestone
  plums, pitted and halved

½ cup crushed almonds
1 teaspoon cinnamon
2 tablespoons sugar

Roll butter dough thick and pat into a 10-inch-by-14-inch pan. Arrange halves of plums, skin side down, evenly over the dough. Combine the crushed almonds, cinnamon, and sugar, and sprinkle evenly over and between the plums. Bake at 350 degrees for 30 minutes.
Serves 12.

APPLE TORTE

Basic butter dough (see p. 116)
1 *egg*
¼ *cup water*
2 *pounds apples, peeled and sliced*

1 *cup sweet wine*
2 *tablespoons sugar*
1 *cup seedless raisins*
½ *teaspoon cinnamon*
Grated rind of 1 *lemon*

Divide butter dough in half, reserving half for the top. Roll bottom dough ¼ inch thick and place in large tart pan. Beat egg and add water. Brush bottom dough with this egg wash. Arrange sliced apples on top of dough. Mix wine and sugar together; add raisins, cinnamon, and grated lemon peel. Pour evenly over the apples. Roll remaining dough into a rectangle, cut into long strips, and arrange criss-cross fashion over top of apples. Brush dough with egg wash. Bake for 40 minutes at 350 degrees.
Serves 8.

APRICOT TORTE

Basic butter dough (see p. 116)
½ *pound apricots,* peeled and pitted, or* 1 1-*pound can*

2 *cups sugar*
½ *cup water*

* If you use fresh apricots, place them in a colander and pour boiling water over the fruit to soften them.

Roll dough ½ inch thick and pat into tart pan. Drain apricots and cook with sugar and water until thick and foamy. Cool. Spread over dough. Bake at 350 degrees for 30 minutes.
Serves 8.

LEMON TORTE

Basic butter dough (see p. 116)
10 egg yolks
2 cups sugar
Juice of 2 lemons
Grated rind of 2 lemons
½ cup chopped almonds
10 egg whites, stiffly beaten

Prepare basic butter dough, roll out thin, and pat into a 10-inch-by-14-inch pan. Bake for 15 minutes at 350 degrees. Meanwhile, beat egg yolks with sugar. Add the lemon juice and rind. Add chopped almonds. Fold in beaten egg whites and pour into half-baked tart, returning quickly to the oven for an additional 15 minutes of baking.
Serves 8.

CARROT CAKE

1 cup sweet butter
2 cups sugar
4 eggs
2½ cups sifted flour
2 teaspoons baking powder
1 teaspoon baking soda
1 teaspoon cinnamon
Juice and rind of 1 lemon
Juice of 1 orange
1 pound carrots, scraped and grated
1 cup broken walnuts
1 cup seedless raisins

Cream butter and sugar. Add slightly beaten eggs. Sift flour, baking powder, and baking soda together. Add to batter gradually. Add cinnamon, lemon rind and juice, and orange juice.

Add grated carrots, broken walnuts, and raisins. Bake in a greased angel food pan for 45 minutes at 350 degrees.
Serves 10.

STIRRED CHERRY CAKE

½ *pound sweet butter,*
  softened
3 *slices white bread, soaked*
  in milk and squeezed
6 *egg yolks*
¼ *cup crushed almonds*

1 *teaspoon cinnamon*
1 *tablespoon sugar*
Grated rind of 1 lemon
6 *egg whites*
2 *cups sweet cherries, pitted*
¼ *cup bread crumbs*

Cream butter. Add soaked white bread. Add egg yolks and beat smooth. Add crushed almonds, cinnamon, and sugar. Add grated lemon rind. Beat egg whites stiff and fold into batter. Add cherries. Pour batter into buttered, bread-crumbed pan and bake for 35 minutes at 350 degrees.
Serves 12.

COFFEE CAKE

¼ *pound sweet butter*
1 *cup sugar*
2 *eggs*
2 *cups sifted flour*

1 *teaspoon baking powder*
1 *teaspoon baking soda*
1 *cup sour cream*
1 *teaspoon vanilla*

Topping:
½ *cup sugar*
2 *teaspoons cinnamon*

1 *cup chopped nuts*
1 *tablespoon melted butter*

Mix ingredients for topping together and set aside. Cream butter and sugar until light and fluffy. Add well-beaten eggs. Sift flour,

baking powder, and baking soda together. Add dry ingredients to batter alternately with sour cream. Add vanilla. Spread half the batter in a 7-inch-by-11-inch loaf pan, sprinkle half of the topping over the surface, then add the rest of the batter and top with the rest of the sugar-nut mixture. Bake at 350 degrees for about 30 minutes, or until browned.
Serves 8.

SOUR CREAM COFFEE CAKE

½ *pound butter*
1 *cup sugar*
2 *eggs*
2 *cups sifted flour*
¼ *teaspoon salt*

1 *teaspoon baking powder*
1 *teaspoon baking soda*
1 *cup sour cream*
1 *teaspoon vanilla*

Topping:
1 *teaspoon sugar*
1 *teaspoon cinnamon*

¼ *cup raisins*
¼ *cup nuts*

Cream butter and sugar. Add eggs. Sift flour, salt, baking powder, and baking soda. Add to batter alternately with sour cream. Add vanilla. Fill 7-inch-by-11-inch pan with batter. Sprinkle topping evenly over batter. Bake at 350 degrees for 30 minutes.
Serves 8.

CHOCOLATE HONEY CAKE

½ *cup shortening*
1¼ *cups honey*
2 *cups sifted cake flour*
1½ *teaspoons baking soda*
½ *teaspoon salt*

2 *eggs*
3 *squares unsweetened*
    chocolate, melted
⅔ *cup water*
1 *teaspoon vanilla*

Cream shortening; add honey gradually and beat well. Sift flour, baking soda, and salt together. Add ½ cup of flour mixture and beat until smooth. Add eggs. Stir in melted chocolate. Add 1 cup flour mixture. Slowly add water. Add remaining ½ cup flour mixture. Add vanilla. Bake in 2 greased 9-inch layer pans at 350 degrees for 30 minutes, or until done. Cool and spread with Honey Frosting.

Honey Frosting:

½ cup honey
½ cup butter
1 teaspoon vanilla
2 egg whites

1 cup confectioners' sugar, sifted
1 square unsweetened chocolate, melted

Cream honey and butter. Stir in vanilla. Beat egg whites until it forms soft peaks. Add confectioners' sugar gradually and beat well. Fold egg whites into honey mixture. Add melted chocolate to ⅓ of frosting and use as filling between cake layers. Spread remaining white frosting on top and sides of cake.
Serves 8.

MATZO HONEY CAKE

6 eggs, separated
1 cup sugar
⅓ cup honey
⅓ cup orange juice
1 tablespoon grated lemon rind

1 tablespoon lemon juice
½ cup matzo cake flour
½ cup potato starch
¼ teaspoon salt

Beat egg yolks. Add sugar, honey, orange juice, lemon rind, and juice. Blend in matzo cake flour. Blend in potato starch. Beat egg whites and salt until stiff. Fold into batter. Line a 7-inch-by-

11-inch loaf pan with waxed paper and fill with batter. Bake at 350 degrees for 1 hour.
Serves 8.

CHOCOLATE MOCHA CAKE

1 *cup sweet butter*
2 *cups sugar*
4 *eggs, separated*
2 *cups sifted flour*
2 *teaspoons baking powder*
2 *teaspoons instant coffee*

1 *cup dry cocoa*
½ *cup milk*
1 *teaspoon vanilla*
1 *cup walnuts, broken into small pieces*

Cream butter and sugar together. Add beaten egg yolks. Sift flour, baking powder, coffee, and cocoa together. Add alternately to the batter with the milk. Add vanilla. Add walnuts. Beat egg whites stiff and fold into the batter. Bake in a greased 7-inch-by-11-inch pan for 45 minutes at 350 degrees.
Serves 10.

CHOCOLATE POTATO CAKE

⅔ *cup sweet butter*
2 *cups sugar*
4 *eggs, slightly beaten*
1 *cup hot mashed potatoes*
1 *teaspoon vanilla*
2 *cups sifted flour*
½ *cup cocoa*

3 *teaspoons baking powder*
½ *teaspoon salt*
½ *cup milk*
1 *teaspoon cinnamon*
1 *teaspoon nutmeg*
1 *cup chopped walnuts*

Cream butter and sugar. Add eggs and beat well. Add mashed potatoes. Add vanilla. Sift flour, cocoa, baking powder, cinnamon, nutmeg, and salt together. Add to batter alternately with milk. Add walnuts. Bake in a 7-inch-by-11-inch loaf pan at 350 degrees for 50 minutes.
Serves 8.

RAISIN CAKE

¼ pound sweet butter
1¼ cups sugar
3 eggs, separated
1½ cups flour

1½ teaspoons baking powder
1 teaspoon vanilla
1 teaspoon lemon juice
½ cup seedless raisins

Cream butter and sugar. Add beaten egg yolks. Sprinkle 1 table-spoon of the flour over raisins, and set aside. Add rest of flour, baking powder, vanilla, and lemon juice to creamed mixture. Beat egg whites stiffly; fold into batter. Add floured raisins. Bake in pan 4½ inches by 8½ inches by 3 inches, at 350 degrees for 30 minutes.
Serves 6–8.

PEACH CAKE

1 tablespoon sweet butter
2 cups flour
3 tablespoons sugar
2 teaspoons baking powder
3 tablespoons sweet cream
1 egg

1 large can sliced peaches,
     drained
2 teaspoons sugar
½ teaspoon cinnamon
1 tablespoon butter

Cut the butter into the flour, sugar, and baking powder until crumbly. Combine the sweet cream and egg, and add to flour mixture, forming into a large ball. Pat dough into a shallow 7-inch-by-10-inch pan. Spread with a layer of sliced peaches. Sprinkle with sugar and cinnamon, and dot with butter. Bake at 350 degrees for about 30 minutes.
Serves 6–8.

PEACH KUCHEN

2 cups enriched flour, sifted
2 tablespoons sugar
½ teaspoon baking powder
½ teaspoon salt
½ cup sweet butter

6 canned peach halves
½ cup brown sugar
1 teaspoon cinnamon
2 egg yolks
1 cup heavy cream

Combine flour, sugar, baking powder, and salt. Cut in butter until mixture is mealy. Grease a 9-inch-square pan and sprinkle bottom and sides with the mealy dough mixture, patting into place. Place peaches cut side up over dough. Sprinkle with brown sugar and cinnamon. Bake in 400-degree oven for 15 minutes. Remove and pour combined egg yolks and heavy cream over top of peaches. Return to oven for an additional 30 minutes. Serves 9.

CRUMB CAKE

2 cups sifted cake flour
2 cups brown sugar
½ cup shortening
1 egg, beaten

½ cup sifted cake flour
2 teaspoons baking powder
1 teaspoon cinnamon
¾ cup milk

Rub 2 cups flour, brown sugar, and shortening together until crumbly. Set aside ½ cup of this mixture to sprinkle over the top of the cake. To the remainder, add the beaten egg, and the ½ cup flour and baking powder. Add cinnamon and milk. Spread batter in a greased 9-inch round or square cake pan. Sprinkle reserved crumbs over the top and bake in a 350-degree oven for 35 minutes. Serves 8.

APPLE-MATZO CRUMB CAKE

2½ cups matzo meal
6 tablespoons sugar
1 tablespoon cinnamon
¾ cup melted sweet butter

3½ cups applesauce
¾ cup seedless raisins
½ cup chopped walnuts
½ teaspoon ground ginger

Mix matzo meal, sugar, and cinnamon. Blend in melted butter thoroughly. Brown in a moderate oven (350 degrees) for 15 minutes, stirring occasionally to keep crumbly. Press ¾ of mixture firmly on the bottom and to 1½ inches up the sides of a 9-inch spring-form pan. Mix applesauce, raisins, and nuts. Pour into pan and spread evenly. Top with remaining crumb mixture and sprinkle with ginger. Bake at 350 degrees for 1 hour. Cool at least 1 hour before removing side of pan. Serve warm or cold, plain or with whipped cream.
Serves 8.

BUTTER NUT CAKE

¾ cup sweet butter
1¼ cups sugar
2 eggs, beaten
1 cup sour cream

1 teaspoon vanilla
2 cups sifted flour
1 teaspoon baking powder
½ teaspoon baking soda

Topping:
¾ cup chopped walnuts
4 tablespoons sugar

1 teaspoon cinnamon
1 tablespoon powdered sugar

Make topping by combining nuts, sugar, and cinnamon, and set aside. Cream the butter and sugar. Add the beaten eggs. Add the sour cream and vanilla. Sift flour, baking powder, and baking soda together; add gradually to batter. Spoon half of the batter into a lightly greased angel food tube pan. Sprinkle half of the topping mixture over the batter, then spoon remaining batter into pan and add remaining topping. Bake at 350 degrees for

55-60 minutes. Sift or shake powdered sugar through strainer over cake while cake is still hot.
Serves 10.

CHOCOLATE SOUR CREAM CAKE

½ *cup dry cocoa*
½ *cup boiling water*
½ *cup sugar*
¼ *pound sweet butter*
1 *cup sugar*
2 *eggs*

1 *teaspoon vanilla*
2 *cups flour*
1 *teaspoon baking soda*
¼ *teaspoon salt*
¾ *cup sour cream*
¼ *cup milk*

Mix cocoa into boiling water; add ½ cup sugar and cool. Cream butter, add 1 cup sugar, mixing well. Add slightly beaten eggs. Add vanilla. Add cooled cocoa mixture.

Sift flour, baking soda, and salt. Combine sour cream and milk. Add dry ingredients to the batter alternately with sour cream and milk mixture. Pour into a greased 4½-inch-by-13-inch loaf-pan and bake at 350 degrees for 40 minutes.
Serves 8.

CHEESE CAKE

6 *eggs, separated*
1 *pound cream cheese*
1 *pint sour cream*
1 *cup sugar*

3 *tablespoons flour*
1 *teaspoon vanilla*
2 *tablespoons lemon juice*

Beat yolks. Add mashed cream cheese. Add sour cream, sugar, and flour. Add vanilla and lemon juice. Beat whites until stiff peaks form, and fold into batter, gently but thoroughly. Grease bottom of a 10-inch spring-form pan lightly; fill with batter. Bake in a 300-degree oven for 1 hour, then turn off heat but do not open door for 1 more hour. When cheese cake is cool, refrigerate until serving time. This recipe produces a high, firm, creamy-textured cheese cake.
Serves 10.

SPONGE CAKE

4 *egg yolks*
1 *cup sugar*
¾ *cup sifted flour*

Grated rind of 1 *lemon*
4 *egg whites, stiffly beaten*
2 *tablespoons sugar*

Beat egg yolks until lemon-colored. Beat in 1 cup of sugar. Add flour and grated lemon rind. Mix well. Fold in stiffly beaten egg whites. Grease 9-inch angel food pan or 4½-inch-by-13-inch loaf pan. Sprinkle with sugar. Heat pan in 350-degree oven for a minute. Pour batter in and bake for 30 minutes at 350 degrees. Remove and invert pan on a cake rack for 1 hour to cool. *Serves* 8.

STRAWBERRY ICING

1 *egg white*
½ *cup sugar*

¾ *cup fresh strawberries,*
washed and hulled

Beat egg white until frothy, adding sugar gradually; continue beating until stiff peaks form. Add fresh strawberries. Spread on sponge cake, or any plain cake. Excellent frosting for Passover cakes.

ORANGE SPONGE CAKE

4 *eggs, separated*
1 *cup sugar*
Juice of 1 *orange*

1 *cup flour*
1 *teaspoon baking powder*

Beat egg yolks until lemon-colored. Add sugar and beat. Add orange juice. Add flour and baking powder. Mix thoroughly. Beat egg whites until stiff peaks form. Fold egg whites into batter.

Bake in an ungreased 9-inch angel food pan or 4½-inch-by-13-inch loaf pan for 30 minutes at 325 degrees. Remove from oven and invert on a cake rack for 1 hour to cool. *Serves* 8.

PASSOVER SPONGE CAKE

6 *eggs, separated*
1 *whole egg*
1½ *cups sugar*
2 *tablespoons lemon juice*
Grated rind of 1 *lemon*

1 *cup sifted potato starch*
½ *teaspoon salt*
½ *teaspoon nutmeg*
Confectioners' sugar (optional)

Beat egg yolks and whole egg together until foamy. Beat in sugar. Add lemon juice and lemon rind. Sift potato starch and salt; add to egg yolk batter. Add nutmeg. Beat egg whites until stiff. Fold into the batter. Grease bottom only of a 10-inch spring-form pan. Fill with batter. Bake in 350-degree oven for 35 minutes, or until cake is firm in center. Cool upside down before removing side of spring-form pan. Dust with confectioners' sugar if desired.
Serves 10.

BUTTERMILK POUND CAKE

½ *cup sweet butter*
2½ *cups sugar*
4 *eggs*
3 *cups sifted flour*
½ *teaspoon baking soda*

1 *cup buttermilk*
1 *teaspoon vanilla*
2 *tablespoons grated lemon peel*

Cream butter; add sugar. Beat in eggs one at a time. Sift the sifted flour with the baking soda. Add alternately with the buttermilk to the batter. Add vanilla. Add lemon peel. Bake in a greased, floured 10-inch angel food tube pan at 350 degrees for 1 hour. *Serves* 8–10.

CREAM CHEESE POUND CAKE

3 *ounces cream cheese*
¼ *pound sweet butter*
1 *cup sugar*
3 *eggs*

1 *cup sifted cake flour*
1 *teaspoon vanilla*
Grated rind of 1 lemon

Cream the cheese and butter together. Add sugar and cream well. Add eggs one at a time. Add flour. Add vanilla and grated lemon rind. Pour into a greased and floured 4½-inch-by-8½-inch loaf pan. Bake at 350 degrees for 50 to 60 minutes. *Serves* 8.

Notice that the pie dough recipe below has an unusual liquid ingredient—orange juice. It gives the crust a delicate flavor and is especially good with the cherry filling. My dear niece, Barbara, gave me the recipe and it gives me great pleasure to include it here.

CHERRY PIE

Crust:
2 *cups flour*
1 *teaspoon salt*

⅔ *cup shortening*
5 *tablespoons orange juice*

Combine flour and salt. Cut shortening into flour mixture. Add orange juice. Work quickly and gently into a dough. For a 2-crust pie, divide dough in half and roll out each half on a floured board.

Filling:

2 *cups fresh sour cherries,*
  pitted
2 *tablespoons quick-cooking*
  tapioca

1 *tablespoon lemon juice*
½ *cup sugar*
½ *teaspoon cinnamon*

Place cherries in a small deep bowl. Combine tapioca, lemon juice, sugar, and cinnamon. Mix gently through the cherries and let stand for 10 minutes. Fill a 9-inch pie shell, cover with second crust, prick top crust with a fork to let steam escape, and brush top with milk. Bake in a 350-degree oven for about 45 minutes, or until crust is lightly browned.
Serves 6.

DATE-CHEESE PIE

Crust:

1 *cup matzo meal*
1 *teaspoon cinnamon*
2 *tablespoons sugar*

⅛ *teaspoon salt*
¼ *cup melted sweet butter*

Blend matzo meal, cinnamon, sugar, and salt. Work in melted butter until thoroughly blended. Press into a 9-inch pie pan and bake in a moderate oven (375 degrees) for 15 minutes. Cool.

Filling:

3 *eggs*
2 *cups cream-style cottage*
  cheese
⅓ *cup light sweet cream*
⅓ *cup sugar*
¼ *teaspoon salt*
1 *tablespoon cornstarch*

1 *tablespoon lemon juice*
½ *cup chopped dates*
1½ *teaspoons grated lemon*
  rind
3 *tablespoons blanched,*
  slivered almonds

Beat eggs until light and fluffy. Gradually beat in the cottage cheese, sweet cream, sugar, salt, cornstarch, and lemon juice until well blended. Sieve mixture through a medium strainer. Beat until smooth. Stir in chopped dates and lemon rind. Pour into cooled pie shell. Sprinkle with slivered almonds. Bake in a moderate (350-degree) oven for 40 minutes or until firm in center. Turn off heat; open oven door slightly and allow to cool in oven for 1 hour. Chill thoroughly before serving.
Serves 6.

CREAM CHEESE PIE

1 *pound cream cheese*   1 *teaspoon vanilla*
2 *eggs, beaten*   *Pinch of salt*
⅓ *cup sugar*   1 *unbaked* 10-*inch pie shell*

Mash cream cheese well, add beaten eggs, and mix until smooth. Add sugar, vanilla, and salt. Pour into unbaked pie shell. Bake in a 350-degree oven for 35 minutes. Cool for 10 minutes and add topping.

Topping:
1 *pint sour cream*   1 *teaspoon vanilla*
⅓ *cup sugar*

Beat sour cream, sugar, and vanilla together. Spread on top of pie, and return pie to oven for 10 minutes more.
Serves 6–8.

SOUR CREAM PIE

Dough:
⅓ *cup sweet butter, or*   ¼ *teaspoon salt*
  shortening   2 *tablespoons cold water*
1 *cup flour*

Combine butter, flour, salt, and cold water into a dough. Roll out to fit an 11-inch pie pan. Fit into pan.

Filling:

1 *cup sugar*
2 *tablespoons flour*
1 *teaspoon cinnamon*
1 *teaspoon nutmeg*

¼ *teaspoon salt*
3 *eggs, beaten*
1 *cup sour cream*
½ *teaspoon vanilla*

Combine sugar, flour, cinnamon, nutmeg, and salt. Beat eggs, sour cream, and vanilla together; add to sugar-flour mix. Beat well. Pour into prepared pie crust. Bake at 375 degrees for 10 minutes, then lower heat and bake at 300 degrees for 40 minutes. *Serves* 8.

CRUNCHY LEMON VELVET

Crust:

½ *cup sweet butter*
½ *cup brown sugar*

1¼ *cups matzo meal*
1½ *cups shredded coconut*

Cream butter and sugar together until light and fluffy. Add the matzo meal and blend thoroughly; add coconut. Place half of this mixture in the bottom of an 8-inch-by-8-inch pan. Pour in filling; top with remaining crust mixture. Bake in a 400-degree oven for 25 minutes, or until top is golden. Chill. Cut into squares.

Filling:

1 *cup sugar*
5 *tablespoons cornstarch*
½ *teaspoon salt*
2⅔ *cups milk*
2 *eggs, beaten*

½ *cup lemon juice*
1 *teaspoon grated lemon rind*
2 *tablespoons sweet butter*
½ *teaspoon vanilla or almond extract*

Combine sugar, cornstarch, and salt in a saucepan. Gradually add the milk. Cook over low heat until thick, stirring constantly. Mix eggs and lemon juice and stir in a little of the hot mixture. Stir this mixture into the mixture in the saucepan. Cook and stir over low heat for 2 minutes. Remove from heat and add grated lemon rind, butter, and extract.

Makes 12 squares.

SESAME-NUT TORTE

4 *eggs, separated*
1 *cup sugar*
½ *teaspoon almond extract*
1 *cup matzo meal*
¼ *teaspoon salt*

1 *teaspoon baking powder*
¾ *cup coarsely chopped walnuts*
¼ *cup sesame seeds*

Beat egg whites until stiff but not dry. Beat egg yolks with sugar and almond extract until thick. Mix matzo meal with salt and baking powder. Fold egg yolk mixture, matzo meal mixture, nuts, and sesame seeds into egg whites. Pour into an ungreased 9-inch round pan which has been lined with waxed paper. Bake in a 325-degree oven for 1 hour. Cool in pan. Cut into portions and serve with ice cream or sherbet. If desired, two layers of the torte may be put together with a layer of softened ice cream in the center.

Serves 8.

PRUNE TORTE

¼ *pound sweet butter*
½ *cup sugar*
2 *eggs*
2¾ *cups sifted flour*
1 *teaspoon baking powder*
1 *tablespoon orange juice*

1 *tablespoon lemon juice*
1 *tablespoon grated orange rind*
1 *tablespoon grated lemon rind*

Cream butter and sugar well. Add eggs. Sift flour and baking powder; add to batter alternately with juices. Add grated rinds. Roll out thick, reserving about ¼ of the dough for a criss-cross topping, and press into an 8-inch-by-12-inch pan, bringing dough all the way up the sides.

Filling:

1 *pound raw prunes, pitted*	½ *teaspoon cinnamon*
½ *cup chopped nuts*	1 *egg*
½ *cup raisins*	1 *tablespoon water*
2 *tablespoons sugar*	

Chop prunes, nuts, and raisins together. Add sugar and cinnamon. Fill the torte shell with this mixture. Roll out remaining dough and cut in strips. Arrange the strips criss-cross over the top of the filling. Brush strips with an egg beaten with water. Bake at 350 degrees for about 35 minutes, or until browned.
Serves 8.

STRUDEL DOUGH

2 *cups flour*	1 *tablespoon cooking oil, very*
1 *egg*	*fine variety*
½ *cup water*	⅛ *teaspoon salt*

Sift flour onto the center of a large pastry board. Separately, beat egg, water, oil, and salt together. Pour this egg mixture into the center of the flour, stirring quickly as you pour. Knead dough lightly but well. Place in a warmed bowl and cover with a towel, resting the dough for about ½ hour. Then, roll the dough on a larger, lightly floured board° until very thin but unbroken. Stretch the dough further by placing the back of your hands

° Or use a sheet, folded several times, placed on a table and floured.

under the dough and gently stretching and pulling the dough outwards all around from center, until the dough is as thin as possible but still unbroken, returning the dough carefully to the floured board after each stretch. Proceed with one of the following fillings.

Serves 10–12.

APPLE STRUDEL

4 *large apples, peeled and thinly sliced*
1 *cup seedless raisins*
½ *cup coarsely chopped walnuts*

1 *cup sugar*
1 *teaspoon cinnamon*
¼ *cup margarine*
Strudel dough (see p. 137)
3 *tablespoons bread crumbs*

Combine sliced apples, raisins, and chopped walnuts. Add sugar and cinnamon. Spread along one long edge of rolled-out rectangle of strudel dough. Dot with margarine. Sprinkle remaining area of dough with bread crumbs. Roll up and bake on greased cookie sheet in 375-degree oven for 35 to 45 minutes.

Serves 10–12.

CHEESE STRUDEL

2 *eggs*
½ *cup sugar*
1 *pound cream cheese*
1 *cup sour cream*

1 *teaspoon vanilla*
½ *teaspoon cinnamon*
½ *cup seedless raisins*
Strudel dough (see p. 137)

Beat eggs and sugar together until lemon-colored. Add cream cheese, softened to room temperature. Add sour cream, vanilla, and cinnamon. Beat well. Stir in raisins. Spread on rolled-out

strudel dough, roll up, and bake on greased cookie sheet at 375 degrees for 50 minutes.
Serves 10–12.

CHERRY STRUDEL

4 *cups canned pitted*
   sour red cherries
1 *cup sugar*
Grated rind of 1 *lemon*
½ *cup chopped almonds*

½ *teaspoon cinnamon*
Strudel dough (see p. 137)
3 *tablespoons bread crumbs*
1 *tablespoon confectioners'*
   sugar (optional)

Combine drained cherries with sugar. Add grated lemon rind, chopped almonds, and cinnamon. Spread along one edge of rolled-out rectangle of strudel dough. Sprinkle bread crumbs over remaining area of dough. Roll up and bake on greased cookie sheet at 375 degrees for 45 minutes. Dust top with confectioners' sugar if desired.
Serves 10–12.

RAISIN-NUT STRUDEL

2 *cups coarsely chopped*
   walnuts
2 *cups seedless raisins*
1 *cup sugar*
1 *teaspoon cinnamon*

Grated rinds of 2 *lemons*
   and 1 *orange*
¼ *cup margarine*
Strudel dough (see p. 137)
3 *tablespoons bread crumbs*

Combine walnuts, raisins, sugar, and cinnamon. Add rinds of lemons and orange to mixture. Spread along one edge of rolled-out rectangle of strudel dough. Dot with margarine. Sprinkle remaining area of dough with bread crumbs. Roll up and bake on greased cookie sheet in 375-degree oven for 35 to 45 minutes.
Serves 10–12.

MANDELBRÖT

3 *eggs*
¾ *cup sugar*
¾ *cup oil*
1 *teaspoon baking powder*

2½ *cups flour*
¼ *teaspoon salt*
1 *teaspoon vanilla*
½ *cup chopped almonds*

Beat eggs and sugar together until lemon-colored. Add oil. Add baking powder, flour, and salt. Add vanilla and chopped almonds. Blend well into a soft dough. With floured hands, shape dough into 2 long loaves, about 3 inches wide and 1 inch high. Place the loaves on a greased cookie sheet and bake at 350 degrees for about 45 minutes. Remove from oven, cut into ½-inch slices, and return to oven to toast for 10 minutes.
Makes about 3 dozen slices.

My family ate challah after challah until one met with their unanimous approval. Old-fashioned balabustas, who baked a Sabbath loaf every week, had many tricks for braiding the bread. Some used multiples of five, seven, nine, and even fifteen strands, magically woven into an oval loaf. The triple layer of three strands each, used in the recipe below, produces the same appearance and is easier for the novice to master. Remember to brush the surface with egg white after the three braids have been assembled in tiers; if the tiers are glazed separately they will slip apart. Nothing says "I care" as loudly as fresh-baked bread.

CHALLAH

1 ¼ -*ounce package dry yeast*
¾ *cup warm water*
2 *tablespoons light cooking oil*
2 *teaspoons salt*

2 *tablespoons sugar*
3 *eggs*
4 *cups flour*
Poppy seeds (optional)

Dissolve yeast in warm water. Let it sit for 5 minutes. Add oil, salt, and sugar. Separate 1 egg, reserving the white at room temperature for a final glaze; beat the yolk into the remaining 2 whole eggs. Add beaten eggs to the yeast mixture. Stir in flour and knead on a floured board until firm and elastic. Place dough in a large greased bowl, cover with a plastic bag or a clean cloth, and let dough double in bulk for 1 or 2 hours.

Turn dough out onto floured board and knead again. Divide dough in half; then divide 1 of the halves into 3 sections. With well-floured hands, roll the 3 sections into long ropes; press the ends of 3 ropes together; braid and press the other ends together. Divide remaining half of dough into 2 sections, one larger than the other. Make 2 more sets of braids. You now have 3 braids, in 3 sizes. Place largest braid on greased baking sheet. Place medium braid on top of large one, and smallest braid on top of the medium one. Let loaf stand at room temperature for 1 hour. Then brush with the egg white to get a shiny crust. Sprinkle with poppy seeds if you wish. Bake loaf in a 375-degree oven for 50 minutes, or until golden brown. *Makes 1 large loaf.*

BANANA BREAD

⅓ *cup butter*
⅔ *cup sugar*
2 *eggs, beaten*
2 *bananas, mashed*
1¼ *cups flour*
2 *teaspoons baking powder*

¼ *teaspoon baking soda*
½ *teaspoon salt*
1 *teaspoon grated lemon rind*
1 *teaspoon lemon juice*
½ *cup chopped walnuts*

Cream butter and sugar. Add eggs one at a time. Add mashed bananas (use very ripe bananas). Sift flour, baking powder, baking soda, and salt together. Add gradually to batter. Add lemon rind, lemon juice, and chopped walnuts. Bake in a greased 4½-inch-by-8½-inch loaf pan for 55-60 minutes at 350 degrees. *Serves 8.*

DATE AND NUT BREAD

½ cup raisins
1½ cups dates, pitted and
   cut up
1 cup boiling water
1 teaspoon baking soda
⅔ cup brown sugar

¼ teaspoon salt
1 egg
1⅔ cups flour
1 teaspoon baking powder
½ cup walnuts
1 teaspoon vanilla

In a deep bowl, combine raisins, dates, and boiling water. Stir in baking soda, brown sugar, and salt. Cool. Add slightly beaten egg. Sift flour and baking powder together. Add to batter. Add walnuts and vanilla. Grease 4½-inch-by-13-inch loaf pan. Pour in batter and bake for 45 minutes at 350 degrees.
Makes 8–10 slices.

BAKING POWDER BISCUITS

2 cups sifted flour
1 tablespoon baking powder
½ teaspoon salt

¼ cup vegetable shortening
⅔ cup milk

Sift flour, baking powder, and salt together. Cut in shortening until mealy. Add milk slowly and form a soft dough. Roll on floured board to ½-inch thickness. Cut into rounds and place on greased pan. Bake for 10 to 15 minutes in a 475-degree oven.
Makes 1 dozen.

· 15 ·

*"If thine enemy be hungry, give him bread to eat,
And if he be thirsty, give him water to drink."*

BOOK OF PROVERBS

A Little Fruit, Maybe?

What goes better with a slice of sponge cake than a dish of
stewed fruit? When the meal has been too hearty for a rich cake
dessert, or when the spirit is willing but the appetite is almost
sated, nothing tops things off more gracefully than a fruit compote. Sweet, light, and just right!

There is no end to possible fruit combinations—they can go

on forever as your imagination or your larder dictates. The flavor of canned fruits is improved when they are heated with a dash or two of cinnamon, and perhaps an ounce of sweet grape wine. Baked apples become a triumph with heavy sweet cream poured over the tops. Even common applesauce gains dignity when it is served in long-stemmed glasses and topped with a dollop of whipped cream and a sprinkling of nutmeg.

The few choice fruit recipes in this chapter may inspire you to create even wilder combinations. Just let your sense of taste guide you to new and delicious experiences!

APPLESAUCE

6 *apples*
¾ *cup water*

⅓ *cup sugar*
¼ *teaspoon cinnamon*

Wash apples and cut in quarters, leaving skins and cores intact. Place in a heavy saucepan with water, sugar, and cinnamon; cover tightly and simmer until apples are mushy. Using a food mill, strain the sauce into a bowl. Add additional sugar and cinnamon according to your taste and the sweetness of the apples. *Serves* 6.

BAKED APPLES

4 *large baking apples*
¼ *cup seedless raisins*
¼ *cup brown sugar*
½ *teaspoon cinnamon*

1 *tablespoon lemon juice*
1 *tablespoon butter or*
   margarine

Core apples, leaving bottoms intact. Pare skin down 1 inch from the top. Mix raisins, brown sugar, and cinnamon together. Fill

cores with this mixture. Arrange apples in a baking dish, sprinkle
with lemon juice, and top with butter. Pour water around the
bottom of pan, about ½ inch deep. Cover with baking dish cover
or foil. Bake at 375 degrees for about 40 minutes, or until
apples are soft but still hold their shape. Remove cover and bake
for an additional 10 minutes. Serve hot or cold.
Serves 4.

CHAROSETH
(For Passover)

1 *cup chopped apples* 2 *tablespoons honey or sugar*
½ *cup chopped nuts (walnuts,* ¼ *cup sweet red wine*
  pecans, or almonds) ¼ *teaspoon cinnamon*

Mix chopped apples and chopped nuts. Add remaining ingredients, and mix thoroughly. Serve with traditional Passover
dinner.
Serves 8.

FRUIT-WINE PARFAIT

3 *cups sponge cake, cut into* 1 *cup canned fruit cocktail,*
  ½ *-inch cubes* *drained*
¼ *cup Concord grape wine°* 1 *cup heavy cream, whipped*

In parfait or sherbet glasses, arrange alternate layers of cake
cubes, fruit cocktail, and whipped cream, sprinkling each cake
layer generously with the wine. Chill.
Serves 6.

° You may substitute loganberry, American Malaga, cherry, or black-
berry wine.

PEARS CONCORD

1 #2½ *can Bartlett pears* ¼ *teaspoon cinnamon*
½ *cup Concord grape wine*

Drain pears. Boil syrup until reduced to ½ cup. Add wine to syrup. Add cinnamon. Stir well and pour over drained pears. Chill thoroughly and serve.
Serves 4–6.

STEWED PRUNES

2 *cups large prunes* 1 *tablespoon sugar*
1 *tablespoon lemon juice* *Boiling water*

Wash prunes and place in a pint jar. Add lemon juice and sugar. Cover with boiling water. Screw on lid and let stand for several hours until cool. Refrigerate.
Serves 4.

STRAWBERRY-PINEAPPLE COMPOTE

1 *pint fresh strawberries* ½ *cup sugar*
1 *cup fresh diced pineapple*

Wash and hull berries. Combine berries and diced pineapple. Sprinkle with sugar; shake bowl to coat fruit evenly. Cover and refrigerate for at least an hour.
Serves 6.

DRIED FRUIT COMPOTE

4 *cups assorted dried fruits,*   ¼ *cup lemon juice*
   i.e., prunes, apricots, pears   3 *cups boiling water*
¼ *cup sugar*

Place fruits in a deep saucepan. Add sugar, lemon juice, and boiling water. Simmer 15 minutes, or until fruit is tender. Remove fruit to a bowl and continue cooking syrup to reduce the amount and thicken for an additional 10 minutes. Pour syrup over fruit and refrigerate.
Serves 8.

INDEX